F

MW01198886

A Beginners and Advanced Practical Guide to Enjoy RV Lifestyle, Boondocking Adventures (Holiday Travel or Full Time Retirement Living), Including Cooking and Repair Tips Across USA

James Heberd

Table of Contents

Introduction 6

Chapter 1: Choosing Your Rig 8

RV Options 9

Motorhome 9

Trailer 14

Choosing Your RV 23

Motorhomes.......................................23

Trailers 27

Truck Camper 31

Rent or Purchase?..................................34

Renting 34

Purchasing...37

How much should I spend? 37

Financial Situation 38

Budget 39

New or Used 39

Handiness...40

Where? 41

RV Manufacturers 41

Private Party 42

Buying Your RV 43

Getting the Best Deals 45

Where do I Store it? 49

Chapter 2: Towing and Carrying 51

Weights, Capacities, and Why They Are Important 52

Matching Your RV 54

Weight Distribution and Sway 57

Chapter 3: Setting Up Your Rig 63

Utilities 64

Water 71

Sewage... 73

CATV/Satellite 75

Cellular Service and Wi-Fi 76

RV Supplies 79

Modifications 83

Chapter 4: Your Voyage............................. 93

Pre-trip and Post-trip inspections 93

Towing and Carrying 97

Securing your RV 103

Backing 104

Using Your Utilities 107

Dry Camping, Boondocking, and Dispersed Camping 114

Chapter 5: Everyday RV........................... 120

Everyday RV... 121

RVing With a Pet 125

Getting a Good Night's Sleep 133

Clothing 138

Bathing... 138

Outdoor Activities 140

RV Cooking 141

RV Costs 143

Maintenance and Repair 149

Breakdowns 152

Full-Timing 156

Chapter 6: What to Know, and Where to Go. 164

Choosing a Destination........................... 164

While you are traveling 167

Conclusion 170

Introduction

Congratulations on downloading *RV Camping.*

The following chapters are a deep dive into the RV Experience, presenting topics such as choosing and outfitting it, traveling in it, spending time in it and planning your trips around it. There are plenty of books on this subject on the market, so thanks again for choosing this one. I made every effort to ensure it is full of as much useful information as possible, so please enjoy.

- Chapter 1 dives into the single most weighty decision you are going to make: buying an RV. The entire process is there from a description of the types, to the process of choosing and buying it.

- Chapter 2 brings focus to the technical side of RVing, consisting of topics such as weights, capacities, and why they are important to you, your family, and other motorists.

- In chapter 3 you will learn about outfitting your rig and making modifications. RVs do not come from the factory with anything!

- Chapter 4 presents practical topics such a conducting pre-trip and post-trip inspections, hitching, securing, backing a trailer, and using utilities at campgrounds and when boondocking.

- In chapter 5 I served up the meat-and-potatoes of the lifestyle: living in your RV day-in and day-out including full-time RV living.

- Lastly, chapter 6 walks you through using web-based tools, smart device apps and other technology such as RV GPS units and trucker's atlases to choose a destination, choose the best way to get there, and navigate along the way.

Chapter 1: Choosing Your Rig

Purchasing a rig will be the weightiest decision you are going to make when considering the RV lifestyle. This chapter provides you with the basic information you will need to get started. You will learn the characteristics of each type of RV including their strengths and challenges, the choice between renting versus purchasing an RV including the cases for each, estimated price points for new RVs, where to buy new and used RVs, what the buying process looks like when purchasing a new RV, and where to store the RV once you've purchased it.

RV Options

When it comes to choosing a recreational vehicle, the choices can be overwhelming. There are three types of RVs: motorhome, trailer, and truck camper. The motorhome is driven, so it has all the components (and upkeep requirements) of a powered vehicle in addition to all the components of a recreational vehicle. The trailer is towed behind a powered vehicle, has all the components of a recreational vehicle, and none of the components of a powered vehicle. The truck camper is a self-contained RV carried in the bed of a pickup truck. In the following section, I will unpack each of these types including their variants.

Motorhome

If you own a motorhome, you do not need another vehicle unless you prefer to tow a vehicle behind you for convenience. What all classes of motorhome have in common is they are self-contained and "ready to go" when you get to your site; you do not to set up anything outside. There are three classes of motorhome: A, B, C, and two sub-classes: B+ and Super C.

Class A: The Class A RV sits on a motor coach frame and resembles a large bus used by companies such as Greyhound. It is typically the largest, heaviest, and most expensive motorhome. Gasoline or diesel fuel powers a Class A motorhome. The diesel-powered Class A is often referred to as a diesel pusher because the engine is always in the back, pushing the coach. Diesel is the powerplant of choice when towing heavier loads or powering heavier multiple-slide units (slides are motor-driven modules that extend outward from the RV and expand its living space). The gas-powered motorhome is the powerplant of choice for the so-called weekend warrior, when towing lighter loads (or no load at all), when the unit itself is lighter, and when the goal is to keep cost down (the diesel option comes at a premium of thousands of added dollars and weight). You will always find the powerplant in the front in gasoline-powered motorhomes.

Driving a larger Class A motorhome often requires a non-commercial Class A or Class B license in addition to an air brake endorsement if so equipped. Consult your state for its licensing requirement for the motorhome you are considering.

Super C: The Super C fills a niche between the Class A and Class C motorhome. It is a larger variant of the Class C discussed below, and it sits on a truck chassis and cab frame (Ford F550, Ram 5500, Chevrolet/GMC 550o or higher). A gas or diesel engine powers the unit based upon its size and amenities. Like the Class C, the single most recognizable feature of the Super C is the overhang above the cab. Here are a few quick differentiators: The Super C costs less than a Class A and more than a Class C. In most cases, the Super C can tow less than a Class A and more than a Class C. The

Super C usually has less amenities than a Class A and more than a Class C.

As with the Class A motorhome, your state may require you to obtain a non-commercial Class A or Class B driver's license and air brake endorsement.

Class C: The Class C motorhome occupies the niche between the Super C the Class B/B+ motorhome discussed below. Size-wise it can be as short as twenty-one feet without slides and up to forty-one feet with multiple slides. These units are typically nimbler and more mobile than a Class A or Super C motorhome. The single-most recognizable feature of the Class C is the overhang above the cab where in most cases a bed is found.

The Class C motorhome supplies many of the amenities of the Class A and Super C at a lower cost and footprint. The Class C manufacturer starts with a van or truck chassis and engine combination (that includes the cab) and adds the living quarters section including all the components needed to live the RV life. The Class C is usually gas-powered and in some instance is able to tow other vehicles or trailers when properly equipped. A Class D driver's license is usually enough to drive this motorhome.

Class B+: The Class B+ motorhome is a larger variant of the Class B discussed below. The B+ looks like a smaller version of a Class C RV. What distinguishes this coach is the body itself. Whereas the Class B confines itself within its conventional van body including the cab, the Class B+ *replaces* the van body with a larger fiberglass box behind the cab. People choose the B+ because they want something with more amenities than a Class B and while retaining mobility and fuel economy, but do not want to make the jump to a less-nimble, mobile, and heavier Class C. Driving a Class B+ motorhome does not feel that much different than driving a conventional passenger van.

Class B: The Class B RV is the smallest of the motorhomes, it looks like a large conversion van, and people sometimes refer to it as a camper van.

The manufacturers start with van chassis and add the components needed to turn it into an RV (e.g., heat, water, stove, sleeping arrangements, etc.) without going outside the profile of the van itself. The footprint is much smaller than a Class C, and the emphasis is on mobility. Class B motorhomes typically will not tow anything because of the emphasis on mobility. Solo travelers, duos without children or pets, and weekend warriors usually choose the Class B. Size and prices are typically lower when compared to their larger and pricier Class C brethren.

Trailer

Towable RVs do not have classes as is the case of motorhomes. Nevertheless, there are distinct types of trailer within the segment: fifth wheel, travel trailer, and folding/tent ("popup") trailers. The benefit of a towable RV is you can leave it behind in the campground while you go exploring in your tow vehicle.

Fifth Wheel: This trailer is the granddaddy of towable trailers. What makes this a fifth wheel is the way it connects to the truck/tow vehicle, and it shares that connection method with the familiar commercial tractor-trailer combination. The fifth wheel is the u-shaped hitch that sits over the rear axle(s) of the truck. A set of jaws inside the hitch clamp onto the trailer's kingpin mounted to the trailer's front overhang as it slides into the hitch.

The fifth wheel is a favorite of full-time RVers, and it is the largest, heaviest, most amenity-packed—and usually the most expensive—type of trailer. Because it is larger it has a roomier, more residential feel. It is usually shorter in towed length than its similarly-sized travel trailer cousin because it moves the traditional front bedroom (or in some cases living room) location up into the truck bed and over the rear axle.

Here are two examples to illustrate how lengths compare between fifth wheel trailers and travel trailers.

- Truck and Travel Trailer: You own a twenty-two-foot pickup truck. A twenty-six-foot travel trailer including the front A-frame and hitch coupler will usually be twenty-nine-feet long. Your combined length is fifty-one feet.

- Truck and Fifth Wheel: You own a twenty-two-foot pickup truck. A twenty-six-foot fifth wheel is twenty-six-feet long. Four feet of the trailer is inside the bed of the truck. Your combined length is forty-four feet.

The fifth wheel is nose-heavy because of the kingpin and the frame that supports it. The benefit of being nose-heavy is that it reduces or eliminates the sway that you will frequently experience when towing travel trailers. There is nothing more unpleasant than towing a swaying trailer all day and this is where the fifth wheel truly shines. Fifth wheel trailers also have more storage than other trailers, which makes it a favorite for full-time RVers. Another boon for fifth wheels is their maneuverability; because the pivot point of the trailer is over the rear axle it can be more maneuverable in tight spaces.

Travel Trailers: This trailer is towed behind a tow vehicle. The travel trailer is the most recognizable and common type of towable RV (think of the iconic Airstream). They are the most common because they offer the most variation in length (ten feet to forty feet), weight, amenities, floor plans, construction, and price. A trailer is a box (self-contained living quarters) assembled on a rolling frame. Because of the way they are towed, they usually will not be as large, heavy, or amenity-packed as the fifth wheel.

Travel trailers tend to make choice easier because the tow vehicle dictates the length. Most people base their trailer decision based upon the vehicle they currently own, especially in the beginning. (Note: Do not rely on the model number as a gauge to length, because some manufacturers use the length of the box only, while others will use the bumper-to-ball length. The only way to know for sure is to either consult the manufacturer's brochure or measure it yourself.)

There are many fifth wheel and travel trailers floor plans, but the most recognizable are the bunkhouse, toy hauler, and the couple's coach.

The *bunkhouse* is a favorite of growing families because it sleeps more people by incorporating bunk beds, and convertible couches and loveseats. Some bunkhouse trailers sleep up to ten or more people.

The *toy hauler* is a favorite of outdoorsy people or who carry their riding hobbies with them. There are few things that differentiate a toy hauler. You will find a garage-like area in the back of the trailer where you secure your motorcycles, ATVs, etc. You load and unload these vehicles via the back wall of the trailer that doubles as a spring-loaded ramp. The toy hauler's frame is heavier than conventional travel trailers of equal length. The frame must be heavier to support the added weight of the toys one is carrying. The frame must also be able to support the weight of a generator, a means to carry fuel for the toys, and the larger fresh water, gray water, and black water tanks required when staying in remote locations.

The *couple's coach* is a relatively new floor plan that is gaining popularity due to the increasing number of couples-only buyers. The focus on this trailer is couples, not families. Recliners or a convertible love seat (think grandchildren) supplies limited sleeping arrangements for others. Couples coaches are usually rich in amenities such as residential-feel appliances and cabinets, fireplaces, open floorplans, ample storage, and full-size queen or king-size beds.

Construction varies between towable trailers, which influences weight and price. There are two types of construction: Stick and tin and all-aluminum. In a stick-and-tin trailer, sticks stand for the wood frame, and the tin broadly stands for the covering (which in the past was corrugated tin). Stick-and-tin is the most common construction method, especially in entry-level trailers. It is less costly to manufacture, less expensive to buy, and heavier than all-aluminum construction. The all-aluminum trailer uses aluminum in place of wood for its sticks which makes it lighter than a wood-frame trailer, and more costly to manufacture and buy.

The *folding trailer* is often the entry-level towable RV. For many years they were the smallest and lightest towable RVs until the advent of the ultra-small, ultra-lightweight teardrop travel trailer. They range from less than 1,000 pounds to well over 4,000 thousand pounds. These towable trailers have been known as "popups" because of the clever way in which they create living space. A cap that spans the length of the trailer serves as the roof the trailer. A lifting mechanism raises the roof and attached to it are screen and canvas panels that when fully-raised create living quarters. Shelves then slide out and become bed foundations, converting a closed, 10-foot trailer into an 18-foot trailer. While having some amenities (e.g., heat, cooking, sink) they are noticeably spartan in finer amenities (e.g., televisions, bathrooms, and in most cases air conditioning).

The *A-frame* is a variant of the folding trailer. Whereas the folding camper uses a cap, screen, and canvas panels, the A-frame substitutes hard panels that when set into position create the letter *A*. The benefit of this variant is its security, climate control, and security. What is loses is head room, and many people are not able to stand up in the trailer except in the middle of the trailer.

The hybrid towable trailer is a bringing together of the folding trailer and the travel trailer. Imagine a shorter travel trailer with the folding trailer bed system. The hybrid has hard sides and soft bed ends that hinge out from the body of the trailer. The hybrid offers more amenities than the folding trailer such as a dedicated bathroom, fresh water, gray water (used sink and shower water) and black water (bathroom waste), and more security. The foldout beds open up floor space normally dedicated for sleeping space in the travel trailer, and this makes for a shorter and lighter weight trailer than the travel trailer. As predicted, prices and amenities lie midway between the folding trailer and the travel trailer.

Truck Camper: This RV is the last type of recreational vehicle and it is carried in the bed of a pickup truck. The profile is readily recognizable due to the overhang above the truck cab. This camper is perfect for the ultra-mobile, outdoorsy customer who enjoys remote locations in mind. They sleep 2-4 people comfortably. You can leave a truck camper behind at a location in the same way as a trailer, freeing up the truck for other activities. Manufacturers offer more amenities each year including holding tanks, heat, air conditioning, and slide-outs. They are extremely sensitive to the size and payload of the truck carrying them. They make the entire vehicle top-heavy, so use extra caution to ensure tanks are empty when transiting locations.

Choosing Your RV

There isn't a perfect RV, so your goal should be to choose the type and floorplan that most closely matches the amenities you want and supports the activities you enjoy. What follows below are the pros and cons for each type of RV.

Motorhomes

There are many benefits of owning a motorhome, convenience being at the top of the list. At the end of a long travel day you can pull into your site, shut off the engine, hit a button to automatically level your rig, put out your slides, and relax. You can also do that when you just do not feel like hooking up your utilities because of inclement weather. If you are carrying water, you can take showers and do dishes, and your onboard generator will supply 110-volt AC electricity to run your appliances and gadgetry.

Traveling in a motorhome is especially comfortable for your passengers who may want to nap, make a snack, watch television or surf the web. Motorhomes tend to have a softer ride because of their length and weight. They will soak up mile after bumpy mile while isolating the occupants from the same jolts that make awfully long travel days when pulling trailers. Diesel rigs will ride even better than gas rigs because of their added weight. Already mentioned conveniences such as residential appliances and furnishings feel more like a home than a recreational vehicle.

Nevertheless, there are some downsides with owning and traveling in a motorhome. The most prominent downside is the sheer size of the motorhome. Larger motorhomes are more at home on major and minor highways. If you want to travel the backroads, this may not be the best way to do that. If you own a large Class A or Super C you can have a vehicle length of at least 38-40 feet. If you are towing a passenger vehicle behind you, your towed length is closer to 60 feet. There are many roads that are unpassable for rigs of such length, and there are many campgrounds (especially older ones including National Parks) that limit length as well. Campground choice and route planning are critical disciplines when you own a Class A.

Length isn't the only issue. Height and weight are issues too. Class A and Super C RVs will need to stick to roads frequented by tractor-trailers because these roads can handle the weight and will guarantee clearance up to 13'6". Make sure you know the weight and height of your rig including the AC units. Single-axle RVs are usually safe while drivers of tandem-axle RVs must pay remarkably close attention to these measurements. Consult the Rand McNally Motor Carrier's Atlas to find the most reliable information on road capability and limitations for your size rig.

Motorhomes do not lend themselves to mobility or freedom to explore at your destination. If you like to explore, then plan on the added cost of a towed vehicle (dinghy) and a means to tow it. This is more so with Class A, Super C, and Class C motorhomes. There is more mobility with a Class B/B+, and to get that mobility you will have to stow your camping gear and disconnect from campground services.

An RV is also more susceptible to high winds and winding roads. In the case of wind, your RV is a huge sail, and traveling in high-wind is risky because of that. What is dangerous is crosswinds, because they will push your rig right over. If you are driving directly against, or with, the wind you will only notice worse, or better, fuel mileage.

There are added expenses due to your motorhome being an RV and a vehicle. If you tow a dinghy, you will then inherit double the maintenance and repair requirements (and expense). Class A maintenance and repair can be as expensive as $200 per hour, and everything on a motorhome is more expensive to replace than on trailers or truck campers.

Trailers

Trailers can be a good purchase. They are amenable to every size family. As outlined above, you can buy a teardrop trailer for "just the two of you," a 40-foot bunkhouse to sleep an entire family, and anything in between.

There is a great degree of price variation in the trailer segment, which allows families to choose the manufacturer, brand, and floor plan that suits their budget and taste. The MSRP on a new, 25-foot Forest River Rockwood trailer can be as high as $40,000 and sell for two-thirds of that at the dealer. On the other hand, the same size trailer from Airstream can set you back $75,000 with little dealer discount.

Note: A Short Discussion on Depreciation. The average time of RV ownership, especially trailers, can be as short as 2 years. In most of those cases, people are "trading up" to another unit with more amenities. RV depreciation is something to consider as a cost if you are trading in 1 or more times, especially if it is in that 2-year period. RVs lose most of their value in the first year (30% in most cases), less in the next couple years, and flatten out around year 4-5. What that means to you is that you'll take quite a loss in the trade in if you do it before then, and then you will be starting over. Try to hold on to your RV for 4-5 years, or plan to buy one 4-5 years old if you want to buy one sooner. You can expect to enter the segment at a pretty low price point if you buy used, especially when buying a trailer.

Trailers are convenient because you keep mobility. Once you unhook, unload and set up camp, you still have the use of your tow vehicle to explore. The RV becomes your "home base" for the duration of your stay.

Nevertheless, there are a few downsides to owning a travel trailer.

Trailers can be confining depending upon their length and the presence or absence of slides. In inclement weather, they can feel cooped up in short order. Once you add in people and pets it can get tight.

Towing a trailer can be a white-knuckle experience, especially when traveling through harsh weather. If your tow vehicle-travel trailer combination is not set up correctly, you can be a victim of trailer sway. Unchecked trailer sway will at least wear you out after a full day of towing, or in extreme circumstances be dangerous to you and others on the other road.

Trailers have a steep learning curve compared to their motorhome counterparts. Even if you have never driven a Class A RV before, you will still be fully familiar with steering and backing it because it mimics driving your car. When towing a trailer, you have to be aware of the hinge point of your combination and allowing enough room to clear obstacles. You have to do that too in motorhomes, but for some reason, it is a skill and discipline that is more difficult to learn when towing trailers.

Trailers require knowledgeable set up for safe braking, sway control, and weight distribution. First, many trailers (and all two-axle trailers) require electric brakes and brake controllers. A brake controller communicates to the tow vehicle's computer, and when you apply the brakes, the controller sends an equal signal to apply the trailer brakes as well. You will need to be able to set the gain (sensitivity) as well the amount of braking that the controller will supply. The second setup element in setting up your combination is sway control. Lastly, you will need to set up your hitch to distribute the trailer's tongue weight evenly across all axles. This learning takes time, practice, and patience.

Another downside to trailers is they are limited by the size and capacity of themselves, and their towing vehicles. The dealers are in business to sell RVs, and they have been known to tell hedge on towing requirements. You need to educate yourself on choosing the right trailer based on your tow vehicle's payload and towing capacity. Place more emphasis on payload capacity than on towing capacity. In fact, you will run out of payload capacity before you run out of towing capacity.

Truck Camper

Truck campers have a lot going for them such as mobility, minimal travel limitations, self-containment, reduced learning, and reduced devices needed.

First, truck campers are highly mobile. Because they fit in the bed of a truck, they can go anywhere a pickup truck can go. Second, length, height, weight, or class limitations do not limit them in the same way motorhomes and trailer-tow vehicle combinations are limited. Third, they are designed to be self-contained, meaning the truck and camper can stay together. There is no need to find a spot to park it apart from your truck. You can stop anywhere and park in same the way you would park a car. The biggest benefit of the truck camper is limitless options of camping sites. If you can take your truck there, you can camp there (if it's legal to do so). Another benefit is the reduced learning curve that goes with truck camping (you just need to slow down and be aware of its height). A last benefit is the reduced equipment you will not need: electronic brake controller, weight-distribution hitch, or anti-sway devices. Truck campers are simpler to choose between because there are only 2 lengths: one for 6' beds and another for 8' beds.

As great as truck campers are, they too, have challenges. They are truck size dependent, more so than travel trailers. Do not try to put a camper designed for an 8' bed into a truck with a 6' bed. Also, there are very few options for half-ton trucks. Three-quarter and one-ton trucks are better suited to carry these campers.

Note: Many states require an agricultural or commercial license plate for 1-ton trucks, regardless of their fuel type, number of wheels, or actual purpose for which you use them.

Truck campers do require modification to your truck's bumper, bed, and/or frame depending on the mounting system you choose (Happijac or

Torklift are your choices). Also, truck campers use a 6-pin connector versus the 4-pi, or 7-pin connectors used on travel trailers, so you will need to plan for that installation. You may also need to add suspension components (e.g., air springs, added leaves) and heavier-duty tires to ensure you carry the camper safely.

Truck campers are top-heavy, so you will need to be more aware of the camper's height (usually no higher than a travel trailer) and how that impacts' the truck's handling due to the higher center of gravity (caused by all the weight sitting above the truck's axles). You will need to understand how the combination's weight, when coupled with height, affects the on-road and off-road handling. Also, the added weight and height of the camper will reduce your truck's unloaded fuel mileage (but no worse than a truck towing a travel trailer).

Truck campers are quite unstable when you live in them while they are still in the bed of the truck. If you stop along the way for a nap or for the night, you telegraph your movements to your truck's suspension. It is not like a trailer where you can run down your stabilizers to steady the unit. Expect your truck and camper to rock and roll when you move around in it.

Truck campers can be much more confining than a trailer. The truck's bed length dictates the length of the camper, and they aren't designed to be full-time luxurious units. True, there will be days when you must be inside due to poor weather but expect to feel a little closed in after a few days.

Rent or Purchase?

Renting

This can be an inexpensive way to make the plunge into the RVing. Renting allows you to "try on" an RV class to see if it fits your lifestyle. If you are not sure what type of RV you would like to buy, rent several types and asses and compare your experiences one to another. Once you've found the type, you can rent units from different manufacturers, brands, sizes, and floorplans. More people rent motorhomes, so trailer availability is limited. I surmise the high buy-in cost of the motorhome lends them to testing more than travel trailers.

Another benefit is you are not making payments on and ensuring something that may use only eight to twelve times a year (national average). Further, you will save money on outfitting since what you see is what you get. It's likely that your rented RV will have all the gear needed to camp, so you can save hundreds you would normally spend outfitting your rig. Also, renting means you will not be spending money on modifications, maintenance and repairs, or storage (that may be a moot point if you have the space and flexible zoning).

There are also some reasons you may not want to rent an RV, and since they are the opposite of the above reasons for doing so, I will bring up just a few points. First, because you know it is not yours, you may worry the whole time and fuss over spills and nicks. That can make you a nagging Nellie!

Second, is the questionable maintenance or repair history. Third, you may rent so much that it offsets the costs of ownership. Fourth, you know others of questionable hygiene have eaten from the same plates, used the same bathroom facility, and slept in the same bed. If you are uncomfortable using stuff other people have used, then avoid renting.

Sixth, you must carry everything you wear, use, or eat back and forth so you will spend time loading and unloading. Seventh, if you meet a difficulty your unfamiliarity with the rental RV's systems means you will not be able to fix it, or your rental agreement will not allow you to fix it. Lastly, your travels become inflexible due to having to have the RV back on a certain date or certain time, which does not allow time for an unplanned side trip to see the country's ball of string with the largest circumference (located in Cawker City, Kanas by the way).

Purchasing

Purchasing is the next great step in the RV adventure once you have rented. This is ideal if you like to tinker, modify, and customize. Other plusses are you can take off and travel on a whim, and the only hygiene to concern yourself with is your own. The best case for RV purchase though is you have the cash to support a payment or outright purchase and insurance, and you have the place (or money) to store it.

How much should I spend?

How much to spend starts with price point, and that point starts with the type of RV you have chosen. Your financial situation, your budget, the decision to buy new or used, how handy you are, and how long you intend to keep it will serve as the criteria for your decision.

The Recreational Vehicle Industry Association (RVIA) estimates the following prices for new, off-the-lot RVs:

- $6,000-$22,000   Folding camping trailers

- $6,000-$55,000   Truck campers

- $8,000-$95,000   Travel trailers

- $18,000-$160,000 Fifth wheel trailers

- $60,000-$150,000 Class   B/B+   and   C
  motorhomes

- $60,000-$500,000 Super C and Class A
  motorhomes

The price overlap is due to the variety in class, size, manufacturer, quality, brand, and amenities.

Financial Situation

Your financial situation will answer the most important question of all: Am I ready to buy an RV? Only you can answer this question. Here are some questions to ask yourself. How liquid am I (in other words how big is your cushion?)? Are all my other financial obligations met (yes is better)? Would this purchase stress my finances (no is better)? Do I intend to make payments or buy it outright (outright is better)? How long do I intend to keep it (more than 4-5 years is better)?

Budget

OK, so you are in a sound financial position. How *much* do you want to spend? This can be a lump sum, or a number derived from monthly discretionary funds. It's typical to finance new RVs for 10-15 years and in many cases, you can push it to 20 years. While that keeps payments low, it results in a remarkably high payback over the life of the loan. Also, an RV loan is a simple interest, fixed payment installment, not a mortgage.

New or Used

New: A primary benefit is you enjoy the warranty. The industry norm warranty is twelve months, although Jayco warrants out to 24 months. Another benefit is you get to modify it how you see fit, and do not have to redo the modifications of others. Still yet another benefit is the long-term use you will get from the rig, especially if you plan on keeping it for the long-haul.

Note: The selling dealer is the dealer who completes warranty work; dealers rarely do warranty work for other dealers.

Used: The greatest benefit is it is less expensive. Depreciation is the largest driver of reduced cost. Second, someone else has worked out the bugs and warranty issues. The RV industry is notorious for less-than-optimal quality control.

Handiness

If you are a handy person, buy a used RV, especially if it is a trailer or truck camper. These systems are basic and get more complicated quickly as you move into motorhomes.

Where?

There are three sources when it comes to buying an RV: RV Manufacturers, RV Dealers and brokers, and private parties.

RV Manufacturers

Some offer direct purchase, most do not. Of the ones that do, some will sell less expensively than dealers and others will not. Once you have decided on your type and brand, contact the manufacturer to see if this is a possibility.

Dealers

The benefit of using a dealer is seeing lots of options, especially if there are multiple dealers for the same brand in the same area. Trailers are known for having related products, so look for sister companies (e.g., Rockwood and Flagstaff). Dealers provide one-stop shopping and make the buying process convenient, even down to selecting and installing a hitch on your vehicle.

RV shows are another way to buy a new RV for 2 reasons: (1) choice/variety, and (2) purchase incentives. YOu can see an overwhelming number of types and brands under one room and at one time. If you take pictures and good notes, you will begin to see the differentiators, especially among the types and brands. Pay attention because there will be incentives to move those products. Most RV shows occur in the winter as people being to stir and look forward to spring.

Private Party

Private party means used and very frequently out of warranty. If you are not RV-savvy, educate yourself or take an RV-savvy person with you.

There are many ways private parties advertise (e.g., Craig's list, RV Trader, LetGo, and Facebook Marketplace). If you are flexible, this can work out well in your favor. If you don't mind traveling, search outside your area. If you find something that intrigues you, start a conversation, get a lot of high definition photographs, get the full history, and see if someone you know in that person's area can inspect for you. One last point: Consult a few sources to check the RV's value (e.g. NADA, RV and Camper Bluebook, etc.).

Buying Your RV

The best time to buy is when your life setting is good, and your financial situation is sound. Once those are satisfied, and you have settled on a class (type), brand, floor plan, condition (new versus used), and how much you will spend, you can start the purchase process itself.

Here are a couple of financial tips:

- Have the figure in mind *before* you go shopping and stick to that amount. A common strategy of dealers is to talk payment versus price. Keep them on track with price (I will explain this in more detail a little later).

- Don't emotionally attach yourself to a unit; thousands of RVs come on the market every day. If you lose out on a unit, keep shopping because it is very likely you will find another one just like it pretty quickly.

- Shop interest rates. Dealers make money on the total sale including the interest rate. While it is more convenient to finance through a dealer, it may prove to be more expensive overall because of their "cut" from the interest rate. On the other side of the coin, dealers have access to multiple lenders, so insist on transparency on rates and what the dealers make from those lenders.

- Shop loans if you intend to finance you RV. If you can get pre-approved that is even better because you know what it will cost. Being pre-approved keeps you in check because you will be shopping on price only and the payment discussion will become irrelevant.

- Ensure you see the itemized list *before* you sign anything.

Getting the Best Deals

Shop at low-demand times of the year. This varies with geography. The RV season in Arizona may be opposite the RV season in Pennsylvania. Find out what peak times are for *your* geographic time of year and don't shop during those times. This not only affects price; it also affects availability. When you buy in peak season you may need to order which can take up to eight weeks. You may receive your rig when the season is over!

Monitor dealer and manufacturer websites and note when offer deals or incentives. Also, find out when manufacturers are rolling out their new model year lines. RV model years usually run one year in advance, so if it is 2019 you will find models from 2020 on the lot as well. Manufacturers and dealers strive to keep lots chocked full of the newest model possible, and the way they do that is move "older" units.

Don't be afraid to shop outside your local area if you can save significant money. The cost of going there and picking it up may outweigh the cost of buying locally. Remember the warranty work point made earlier.

In some cases, dealers will post the manufacturer's suggested retail price (MSRP), and then list their price which is usually two-thirds or four-fifths of the MSRP. When a dealer advertises an RV this way, the dealer will budge little in price. In other cases, dealers will list the MSRP only and you will have to dicker with them. The amount you will pay will most likely be fairly close in both scenarios. The former scenario is easier because the price they advertise is the price you pay, and in the latter scenario you will not know the price until you negotiate. More dealers are moving to the former scenario than the latter scenario.

When buying a new RV, the dealer will offer you an extended warranty. If the extended warranty costs you anything, then it is <u>not</u> a warranty, it is an extended service plan. The extended warranty does nothing more than supply an insurance policy on the recreational vehicle to cover defects in materials and workmanship after the manufacturer's warranty has expired. An extended service is plan is neither good nor bad. Your decision to buy one comes down to how handy you are, and how willing you are to pay extra to have someone else fix issues when they arise (and arise they will!). Settle this question *before* you walk onto the dealer's lot.

When you buy your recreational vehicle, you will not usually take it home right then, even if you do buy it right off the lot. The dealer is going to have to prepare it first, which means conducting a pre-delivery inspection, installing the house battery and filling the propane tanks, making sure the systems work correctly, and ensuring it is clean and clear of construction debris. When you take delivery, the dealer will take you through post-delivery inspection (PDI). There are many PDI versions on the internet; print one and take it with you as the dealer demonstrates how to operate every system and component. Check the items off, take photos and video the PDI if time allows. If you have never owned a recreational vehicle, the PDI will be a fantastic source of information as you troubleshoot systems in the future.

Note: Non-premium recreation vehicles do not come with owner manuals per se. What you will receive is a generic booklet that presents in very general ways that manufacturer's vehicle. You will also receive a stack of manuals, guides, and installation instructions for each component installed in your RV from the toilet to the stereo to the awning. The best thing you can for yourself when you buy your RV is to familiarize yourself with the equipment and these documents. Some RV manufacturers (e.g., Newmar, Prevost and Airstream) supply exceptional literature for their units.

Where do I Store it?

Inside or outside?

Indoor storage is the best scenario when it comes to storing your RV. It will protect your RV from the most damaging environmental concern: UV radiation from the sun that degrades paint and rubber. Climate-controlled units keep the temperature constant so they eliminate wear and tear from temperature-related expansion and contraction, thereby extending the serviceable life of your RV. Ambient temperature units are just that, no HVAC so no protection from temperature fluctuation. At least these units keep wind, rain and ultra-violet rays off your rig. Climate controlled units can run as high as $500 per month, ambient temperature units can run as high as $125 per month depending upon the area of country where you live.

The other choice you have is to store your rig outside. Your rig will be exposed to the elements (sun, water, wind) so it is exposed to damage and a shorter serviceable life. You can protect it with a cover (and those can run from $75 up to a $1000 depending on how large or rig you own).

As far as where, you have got a couple choices as well. You can store your RV on your own property if space and zoning allow it, or in a commercial location such as a storage lot. If you keep it on private property you have better control and access, and the downside is, well, it's THERE. You can also store it in a commercial lot. The upside is it is off your property and the downside is less-than-ideal access (travel time and security measures) and increased worry about the increased risk of theft and vandalism. Do not store expensive items in your RV while it is in storage and install high-quality locks on it.

Chapter 2: Towing and Carrying

This chapter focuses on the technical side of RVing. You will learn about weights, capacities, and why they are important. You will also learn about matching an RV to your towed vehicle, tow vehicle, or truck. Lastly, you will learn the ins and outs of using a brake controller, how to set up weight distribution when towing trailers, how to tow a vehicle behind your motorhome, and how to eliminate or reduce trailer sway.

Weights, Capacities, and Why They Are Important

Weights and Capacities

<u>Two Vehicle Ratings</u>

- Curb weight: How much a vehicle weighs from the factory with installed options, full fluids, and no passengers.

- Payload: How much extra weight the vehicle is able to carry (passengers and cargo).

- Gross Vehicle Weight: Curb weight plus payload.

- Gross Vehicle Weight Rating: The maximum allowable weight the vehicle.

- Combined Gross Weight Rating: Maximum weight of a tow vehicle and towed vehicle when connected to each other.

- Gross Axle Weight Ratings: How much weight each axle can carry. This is especially important to watch when towing a trailer.

RV Weight Ratings

- Dry weight: How much an RV weighs from the factory with all options installed and tanks empty. **Note**: Some manufacturers include weight of propane tanks and battery, some do not. Check with your manufacturer to determine the elements of dry weight.

- Cargo Carrying Capacity: The amount of weight your trailer or truck camper can carry.

- Occupants and Cargo Carrying Capacity: The amount of added weight your motorhome can carry.

- Gross Vehicle Weight Rating: The maximum allowable weight of the RV.

- Tongue Weight: the amount of the trailer's weight that is being carried by its tongue (hitch)

Matching Your RV

Motorhome

Many RVers drives their coaches like a car and do not mind the lack of mobility. However, many people tow a vehicle (often called a "toad" or "dinghy") behind the motorhome.

If you are going to tow a vehicle, then you need to ensure your motorhome has a high-enough towing capacity to allow it. Larger motorhomes can tow larger dinghies, and diesel motorhomes can tow still larger dinghies. There are two tactics when choosing a motorhome-vehicle combination. First, know in advance what type of vehicle you are going to tow and buy a motorhome based on that. Second, buy the motorhome and then a tow vehicle based on that motorhome's towing capacity. Many RVers purchase the motorhome first since it is the more expensive purchase.

The next decision is to decide how you will tow your dinghy: dolly, trailer, or flat tow (all four wheels are flat to the ground). Flat towing uses the amount of your tow vehicle's towing capacity, dolly towing uses more capacity, and towing your vehicle in a trailer requires the most capacity. This is because you are adding the weight of the trailer. To compensate you will need to choose smaller vehicles as you move from flat, to dolly, to trailer.

Trailer and Truck Camper

There are two schools of thought as there is with the motorhome: buy your trailer based upon a tow vehicle's capacities or buy a tow vehicle based upon the trailer's weight. The first scenario is more common. See the section below on weight distribution and sway for more information on setting up for safe towing.

The gasoline versus diesel fuel is a much-debated issue among RVers that is not easily-solved by simply weighing pros and cons. The choice often comes down to some intangible aspect that nudges you one way or the other.

Gasoline: A gasoline-powered vehicle is less expensive to buy, less expensive to maintain and repair, is less finicky than diesel, and can carry more payload capacity among equally-equipped diesel vehicles. It also has less torque, lower MPG, lower towing capacity among equally-equipped diesel versions, and lower resale.

Diesel: A diesel-powered vehicle is more expensive to buy, maintain and repair, more finicky, and has a lower payload capacity among equally-equipped gas vehicles. It also has more torque, higher MPG, and more towing capacity among equally-equipped gas vehicles.

From the seat of the pants, expect the gas engine to work more. Manufacturers design RV gas engines to rev because revving equals power and torque. Gas engines will get noisy when they do rev, and you are going to work the gas pedal more to keep the revs in the engine's sweet spot for pulling. A diesel will not work as hard, and you will work the fuel pedal much less.

Class A motorhomes give you little choice. Smaller motorhomes will be gas-powered, and larger ones will be diesel. Dual-axle Class A and Super C motorhomes are diesel only. Class C, B, and B+ are usually gas-powered, the exception being Mercedes-Benz rigs which are exclusively diesel-powered.

Weight Distribution and Sway

Weight Distribution

Leveling is the first part of weight distribution. The goal is a level trailer connected to a level vehicle, because level vehicles keep weight even across all axles. If a trailer is tongue high when connected, the tongue weight shifts weight backward, increasing the tendency for the trailer to sway. A tongue low trailer shifts weight forward onto the tow vehicle's rear axle while unloading its steer axle. One way to level is to add suspension aids such as airbags. Airbags are useful if you use them in conjunction with weight distribution.

Trailers distribute their weight on two points: the axles and the tongue. RV manufacturers design trailers to carry 85-90% of their weight on the axles, and the other 10-15% by the tongue. The hitch is the fulcrum between the tow vehicle and the trailer axle(s) that transfers the trailer's tongue weight to the rear of the tow vehicle. When it applies that weight, the vehicle sags causing weight transfer from the front axle and trailer axles to the tow vehicle rear axle. Undistributed tongue weight loads the tow vehicle's rear axle, unloads the tow vehicles' front axle, and unloads the trailer's rear axle (if a 2-axles unit).

When the front axle unloads the headlights point up (blinding on-coming drivers), reduces tire contact with the ground (which decreases steering and stopping ability), and places added stress onto the rear axle.

When the rear axle of 2-axle trailer unloads it transfers more load to the front axle. That places more stress on the front axle and suspension and increases the load on the front axle tires. The increased tire loading will increase pressure and tire temperature which could cause a blowout from increased heat. Uneven weight distribution also creates uneven braking between the two axles.

When a tow vehicle's rear axle is loaded it can move the payload outside the vehicle's limit, put extra wear and tear on rear suspension components, and result in a "squishy" rear end that can lead to trailer sway.

A weight distribution hitch (WDH) redistributes tongue weight. The goal is to distribute the trailer's tongue weight evenly across the two vehicle's front and rear axles, and the trailer's axles.

The WDH hitch typically uses spring or trunnion bars. One end of the bar connects to the trailer's A-frame (the triangular-shaped area in front of the trailer where the propane tanks and battery are mounted), the other end to the hitch. The bars push upward on the hitch coupler, thereby resisting downward pressure placed on the ball by the tongue weight. The spring/trunnion bars are indexed to the amount of tongue weight redistribution needed: 1,000-pound bars for 1,000 pounds of tongue weight, etc. A WDH can run from a few hundred dollars up to $3,000 at the time of this writing. Most incorporate some form of sway control as well.

Sway

You are towing a large object with flat sides, so you are in effect towing a sail. Every bit of wind will grab that sail and push it around in the same way wind pushes a weather vane. Wind pushing your trailer causes it to sway on its pivot point: the ball. Trailer sway pushes the tow vehicle in the opposite direction the wind is blowing. Trailer sway can create accidents when the sideways motion exceeds the tow vehicle's ability to dampen that sway.

Manufacturers build in sway control in many of today's vehicles, particularly trucks. When sway is detected, the tow vehicle's onboard computer will make suspension changes and brake inputs to counter the sway. The onboard also communicates the change to the trailer when it is connected via the 7-pin connector.

Sway minimizers use some means of friction to reduce trailer sway as it pivots on the ball. Sway eliminators use a complicated system of multiple balls, bars and attachments to project the pivot point from the ball to the area of the rear axle. Sway minimizers are inexpensive, around $75 each side (it is always best use 2). Sway eliminators (that also incorporate weight distribution) start around $1,500 and can climb to $3,000.

Chapter 3: Setting Up Your Rig

This chapter brings out the equipment you will need to buy. RVs do not come from the factory with anything! You will learn about setting up your utilities, outfitting yourself for inside and outside RV living, making modifications to your rig, and ways to enhance security.

Utilities

Electrical System: Campgrounds are notorious for spikey electricity, and the last thing you need is burned-up electrical equipment or a burned-down RV. In the event of power spikes and sags, the surge suppressor and the line conditioner will ensure you are not a casualty.

The *suppressor* is an external accessory that plugs into the pedestal, and the RV then plugs into the suppressor. The role of the suppressor is to suppress spikes in voltage, and I do not the $7.99 version found in big-box stores. You will need at least a 30-amp suppressor for truck campers and many travel trailers, and a 50-amp suppressor for many travel trailers, 5th wheels, and most motorhomes. These suppressors can be quite expensive, starting at around $100 and topping out around $300 depending on the features added. Even inexpensive suppressors are now coming with built-in circuit analyzers to detect issues in wiring as soon as you hook up and turn on the power.

A *line conditioner* does two things. First, it serves as a suppressor and a short-term voltage booster. The suppressor takes care of spikes but does nothing for sags (drop in voltage). When power sags, the volts drop, and the amps go up to compensate. The byproduct of increased amperage is heat. Your equipment (especially the air conditioner) will try to compensate and fry itself in the process. It also supplies a temporary voltage boost. Regardless of what you read on the forums, it does not take extra power from the park pedestal to do this. The line conditioner uses internal circuitry and transformers to keep voltage on hand. The benefit of the line conditioner is that you get two functions in one: suppression and conditioning. If you buy a line conditioner you will not need to buy an added suppressor. Expect to pay upwards of $500 for a quality line conditioner. Line conditioners come in external or internal versions. External versions plug directly into the pedestal, and the RV plugs into the conditioner. In internal versions, the unit is hard-wired into the RV.

Tip: Bring an extra power cord. Parks do not all locate the power pedestal in the same place. It can be in the back, front, or in-between. That could put you in a position of not having enough cord to reach the pedestal. A 25-foot, 30-amp cord will set you back about $50, and a 50-amp cord can be upwards of $100.

Tip: Buy a couple of dog bone adapters of various amperages (and thereby connections). Dog bone adapters allow you to adapt your RVs power connection to a connection of different amperage. For instance, you own a 30-amp rig and the only power available at the pedestal is a 50-amp receptacle. A 50-amp male to 30-amp female adapter will allow you to make that connection. Thirty-amp receptacles are the most common power connection, so often they can be loose and worn out. Buy the 50-amp male to 30-amp female adapter first and add others as needed. Also, if your rig is 50-amp, buy a 30-amp male to 50-amp female adapter first.

Note: A 50-amp receptacle carries 25 amps on each leg, so if you adapt your 30-amp RV to this receptacle you only be tapping into one of the legs, so you will lose 5 amps total.

Solar power allows you to charge your batteries when no power is available. You will need a solar panel, a charge controller, and means to connect the controller to the battery or batteries.

There are a couple of ways to mount panels. You can mount them directly to the roof of your RV or use portable "suitcase" panels. The advantage of roof-mounted panels is they do not have to be set up as is the case with portable panels. Another advantage is they are always charging, even while you are on your way to your next destination. Lastly, with roof-mounted panels, you do not worry about thieves absconding with them. An advantage of portable panels is they are not parking-spot dependent, meaning you can move them around to catch the sun, even if you are under trees (and your cord is long enough). Portable panels also allow you to move them to other locations to charge other things. Panels have different ratings, which means different watt-generating capacity. Figure spending about $1/watt for your panels.

Next, you will need a controller. The controller regulates the charge to the batteries, so they don't get cooked (especially a problem with deep cycle, lead-acid batteries). The controllers do this by monitoring battery voltage and supplying only what the battery or needs. Prices range from about $50 to $1,000 depending upon capability and brand.

Batteries vary from RV to RV. Motorhomes use 2 different types of batteries. The first type is the starting battery. It handles starting the engine and running the motor-vehicle part of the RV. The second type is the house battery that handles running the RV's 12-volt system. Larger motorhomes and diesel-powered motorhomes will carry banks of these batteries. Trailers and truck campers usually carry just one house battery to run their 12-volt systems. If you are going to add solar capability, the first thing you will need to do is replace the house battery. Most RVs come with a 12-volt, marine grade, deep-cycle house battery. Replace that with 2, 6-volt golf cart (deep-cycle) batteries. These batteries have high capacity and will hold more charge for a longer time. Golf cart batteries heavy and expensive, around 60 pounds each and upwards of $200.

Some RVers carry *generators*. Generators come in very handy if power fails, or if you plan to dry camp or boondock. If you buy one, ensure it is an inverter-type generator instead of a contractor generator for two reasons. First, an inverter generator puts out smooth power (sine-wave) for sensitive appliances. Second, it is much quieter than a contractor generator (an all-important consideration for campgrounds that allow generator use during non-quiet hours, usually 8:00 am to 10:00 pm). Generators come in different watt-generating capacity, and most inverter generators have a 15- or 20-amp receptacle in addition to an RV 30-amp receptacle. If you have a 50-amp rig, use your 30-amp male to 50-amp female dogbone adapter.

Note: You can usually run a 13,500 BTU air conditioner on a generator as small as 2000-watts, provided you have upgraded the air conditioner with a part that reduces its required 1,700 startup amperage (e.g., Microaire EasyStart, retail around $300). If you have not upgraded your air conditioner, you will need a generator with more capacity (e.g., 2800-3000-watt generator to start a 13,500 BTU air conditioner, and 3,500-watt generator to start a 15,000 BTU air conditioner). Once the air conditioner starts its watt requirement drops precipitously (600 continuous watts). If you are intending to boondock, I highly recommend the Microaire EasyStart to conserve electricity (where every amp and watt counts).

Motorhomes and upper crust 5th wheels are usually stocked with a generator that is quite powerful, often 8.5k up to about 14k (Onan/Cummins are the primary producers). That is because of the components that require more electricity: residential refrigerators, 15K BTU air conditioner(s), hair dryers, microwaves, and coffee makers are the key culprits. The motorhome's onboard generator allows you to run all these items on the go (except the refrigerator which can run on propane).

Water

Potable Water Hose: Buy a superior quality NSF-approved water hose in one-half inch or five-eighths inch diameters. Consider two lengths of 25-foot hose for hard-to-reach pedestals.

Tip: A five-eighths inch hose provides more pressure than the one-half inch hose, which is more helpful when showering.

Blank Tank Flush Hose: Buy a separate hose for black water tank flushing. Any hose will do, just ensure it is not white, so you don't confuse it with your potable water hose. A black rubber hose is always a good choice because it becomes obvious which is which. Do not store these hoses together and connect the ends when you are not using them.

Water pressure regulator: Campground water supplies fluctuate in pressure. If you have a newer RV the water lines can handle up to 100 PSI, but the safest way to go is to plan for 50-60 PSI. Water pressure higher than that can yield a soggy RV. You can choose either a non-adjustable inline pressure regulator or an inline adjustable pressure regulator. The non-adjustable regulator will set you back around

$10, and the adjustable will set you back about $75. In either case, it is good insurance.

Another helpful water-related accessory is the Camco Water Bandit. You would use it in situations where you try to hook your hose to spigot with stripped-out or nonexistent threads (usually at the dump station). Attach one end to the hose via threads, and the other to the source via the hard-rubber adapter. Do not try to use full pressure because it will push the hose off the spigot. Start with a trickle and add pressure until it pops off. Note that valve position, re-attach the hose and turn the valve to a position just short off the push-off position.

Tip: Keep 2 Water Bandits, one for fresh water and another for black tank rinse. Store them in zip-lock bags.

Sewage

What goes in must come out, and to make that happen you need sewer hoses. Consider 2, 25-

foot sections so you can reach your site's sewer connection whether it is in front, back, or in between.

You will also need adapters to connect the hoses to the sewer pipe itself as well as other accessories. Ensure you have a clear elbow on at least 1 end of the hose so you can see when the tank is empty, especially useful when draining and rinsing the black water tank. Also, consider a clear adapter on the RV side because you can attach your black tank flush hose mentioned in the earlier section directly to the elbow to flush your black tank. Solids left behind in the tank will create unpleasant odors when the RV is closed up (especially in the summer!).

Tip: Buy a latex or vinyl gloves to wear anytime you are handling black water hoses, sewer hoses, and their attachments.

CATV/Satellite

Once upon a time, cable television (CATV) reigned supreme in campgrounds, so you will most likely find a CATV input jack somewhere on your RV, either on the outside skin (usually trailers and truck campers), or the utility bay on 5th wheels and motorhomes. Also, you may see a CATV outlet jack, 110-volt receptacle, and corresponding TV mounting bracket on the door side of the RV for those times when you watch TV outside.

A satellite input jack is becoming common on all types of RVs. One jack means that you are going to have to choose whether you use it for entertainment or data. That line is blurred now with the advent of web-based entertainment such as Netflix, Hulu, and others.

If you are going to use your RV's satellite connection you will need to buy the dish and receiver, and they don't have to come from the same place. The trickiest part of the equation is the antenna. The easiest RV satellite antennas to set up (and the most expensive) are the ones that "set themselves up." The automated GPS unit uses internal circuitry GPS and make azimuth and altitude changes on their own (e.g., Winegard Pathway X2 @ $500). You'll find the highest end automatic units in motorhomes where the system stays locked on the satellites while you are on the move (e.g., Winegard RoadTrip T4 @ $1,300). Manual units are much less expensive (around $200) and you make the azimuth and altitude changes (each time requiring a new scan).

Cellular Service and Wi-Fi

Cellular Service: Some cellular systems pull in and amplify cellular signals that improve reception. The components are an outside antenna, a power supply, a boost module, and an inside antenna. While sharing these components, manufacturers their products in size and capability. In some cases, the phone must either rest on or be near the inside antenna (e.g., weBoost Drive Sleek at around $200). In the case RV systems, the inside antenna is generally good for a 10-foot broadcast range to your phone (e.g., weBoost Drive 4G-X RV @ around $500).

Wi-Fi: A Wi-Fi booster cannot amplify what isn't there, a Wi-Fi booster is just a repeater that receives a campground's Wi-Fi, and re-broadcasts it internally. It consists of a wireless router and antenna module mounted on the roof of your RV. It runs on the RV's 12-volt system. To receive boosted Wi-Fi, start your router, then use its software to connect it to the campground's Wi-Fi router. Next, create an internal network from your installed router, and then connect your devices to the router. Wi-Fi download and upload the speed is dependent upon the capabilities of the campground gateway, what traffic it allows, and how many others connect to it. Just because you have "full" Wi-Fi bars does not mean you will have the same data throughput.

Combination Cell and Wi-Fi Booster: This combines both functions discussed previously into one unit (e.g., Winegard Connect 2.0 WiFi & 4G LTE, around $400 for the unit itself). The combination is a stand-alone unit; you will need a data plan just like a cell phone or cellular service-capable tablet.

Many people build their own systems based upon the components listed above. For instance, some will buy a Pepwave cell receiver/router such as the MAX BR1 Slim @ $300 and build their own MIMO antenna. MIMO means multiple-in, multiple-out antennas and connections that 4G uses to achieve its speeds. The beauty of building your own system is you can create a directional antenna, then you use a device to locate the tower, and then point the antenna in that direction. A directional MIMO antenna is far more receptive versus the unipolar mount that is the norm in mobile applications.

RV Supplies

When it comes to supplies, you are going to load into the RV everything needed for day-to-day living. Think of this as outfitting your RV. Remember, everything you add deducts from the CCC in the case of trailers and truck campers, or OCCC in the case of motorhomes.

There isn't a "rule of thumb" to estimate how much weight you should expect to add when outfitting your RV. The best way to achieve the most accuracy is to either weigh each thing you add or weigh the RV before and after loading. Do not forget to include the weight of the equipment.

Bedroom: Make sure to load enough bedding to allow for change-outs on longer trips. If you like a particular pillow, buy an extra one and keep it in the RV. Don't forget your CPAP/BiPAP if you use one. By the way, more RVs are coming with 110- and 12-volt receptacles by the bed for this purpose, and CPAP/BiPAP manufacturers now offer 12-volt adapters (expect to pay around $100).

Kitchen: When loading cookware, try your best to choose lighter materials and select multitask items to save weight. When it comes to plates, cups, and eating utensils, lighter is better. If this is your first RV, use big-box finds as a baseline and don't forget to pack paper products in the event you are conserving water.

A small broom and mop will be helpful, and you may wish to consider a battery-powered stick vacuum. If you are going to load cooking supplies, ensure they can sustain broad swings in temperature and avoid glass containers when possible because they add weight. Store food items in rodent-proof containers.

Consider compartmentalizing your cabinets. Manufacturers leave a blank slate, and vertical is the best way to use more space. Use nonslip material to keep contents from shifting. Remove pizza stones and microwave turntables and store them during transit to prevent breakage.

Bathroom: Outfit with duplicates from your house so you don't have to carry items back and forth. Use single-ply toilet paper only! Two-ply doesn't degrade and it can clog RV and campground plumbing systems. Consider using vault toilets and shower facilities when available if you are on a longer trip and in a campground without hook-ups. Purchase a black tank treatment such as Camper's Friend and add it to your black tank after you drain and flush it.

Tip: When going number 2, add water to the bowl lay a strip or 2 of toilet paper across the bottom. It makes flushing more efficient and hides the evidence!

Living Area: Add the things you will use in inclement weather (e.g., games, extra blankets, weather radio).

Outdoors

- Animal-proof trash can

- Outdoor carpet

- Outdoor chairs

- Screen room

- Screen shade attachment for RV awning

- Tools to stoke and keep a wood fire

Note: Most states and campgrounds prohibit bringing in your own firewood due to the connection between transported insects in wood and deforestation. Some will allow outside firewood if you bought it locally (and you have proof that is). Campgrounds usually have bundled wood for sale at a reasonable cost. A bundle should last an evening unless you like a hot fire!

- Fire pits: Some campgrounds do not allow wood fires (e.g., Disney World Fort Wilderness), so a propane fire could be a great alternative. Check your campground for prohibitions.

- A coarse bristled brush to clean outdoor shoes, especially when it has been raining. Some people also add shoe hangers to the inside or outside to prevent wearing dirty shoes inside the RV.

- If you have pets bring dog leads and water bowls

- Bug repellant is necessary. Many campgrounds now prohibit citronella candles because of the open flame.

- Outdoor grills are handy because they limit traffic into the RV, they reduce heat buildup and odors that cooking retains, and they offer more work area (especially if a table is close by).

Modifications

We Americans are famous for the way we maintain and manicure our suburban yards. We take that cultural quirk with us when we go camping as well. Most RVers start modifying their rigs immediately. It is *your* space, and it needs to be convenient and aesthetically pleasing to *you*. Modifications consist of simple paint and posters to installation of backup battery systems.

The only limitation is your budget and imagination. The following section presents many of the most common modifications (besides the ones I have already mentioned). The best way to discover useful modifications is to be observant at campgrounds and note what people are doing to their RVs. They will be a major source of inspiration to you as you begin your modification journey.

One of the most common modifications is paint and wall coverings. Recreational vehicles tend to be dark and monotone inside with browns and tans throughout. This helps cover dirt and grime, but it also makes it appear dingy and depressing. Many people paint the inside of their RV a lighter color, especially the cabinets. Manufacturers have caught on to this and are now offering lighter toned walls and cabinets. If you are going to paint anything on the RV's interior, use latex paint because it will not off-gas like oil-based paints. Avoid nails and screws in the walls because manufacturers do not always frame the unit at 16" on center as contractors do in residential homes. Use adhesive hooks proven to work (3M for instance).

Most recreational vehicles are equipped with miniblinds that often either break or bend, and it is common to lose the rod that dims them. An alternative is to remove and replace them with a custom valance and drapes.

A very common interior modification is a change in cabinet and storage use. Cabinets are often a blank slate with only minimal compartment separation, which in turn reduces useful storage. Bins, dividers, and stackable containers are the primary means to keep your stuff from moving around.

A helpful modification for outside the RV is using garden hose carry straps to keep your hoses and power cords well-organized. The straps are also very handy when it comes to carrying heavy 30-amp and 50-amp electric cables.

Another common exterior modification has to do with your RV's sewer hose. For years people would store their sewer hose in the back bumper. That solution worked well then, but today's hoses now have tips with bulky connectors that prevent storing them in the bumper. The hose itself fits, but the connectors do not. There are two solutions for sewer hose storage. The first solution is to ensure you fully rinse the hose and then store it in a large Tupperware-type, covered storage container. You can transport the container in the back of the tow vehicle or in one of the RV's storage compartments. Another solution is to mount five-inch PVC fence posts under the rig (motorhomes and trailers) and store the hoses there.

A favorite modification for those who work remotely is removing the RV's booth or dinette and installing a desk. The desk can do double-duty as a dining table. Another option for working road warriors is to purchase a bunkhouse RV and remove the bunks and convert that space into a workspace. A door separates the bunk rooms from the rest of the coach in some RVs. These are ideal models for office conversion. If you need a larger space, some convert toy hauler garage space into office space.

Arguably the most talked about modification you will find on RV forums is original equipment manufacturer (OEM) tire replacement. To hold the cost down, manufacturers install what forum users call "China bombs" (lower-quality tires manufactured in China). RVers call these OEM tires China Bombs because they have a reputation for blowing out well before they are due to be replaced, causing thousands of dollars of damage to the RV. As a preventive measure many RVers will replace the OEM tires with high-quality tires manufactured in the United States (e.g., Goodyear Endurance, Maxxis 8800, etc.).

Note: The enemy of RV tires is not miles as with passenger car tires. What is deadly to an RV tire is age, exposure to ultraviolet light, and improper inflation. In the case of age, it is because RV tires don't see enough road time to get to their mileage limit. Tires also degrade just by being exposed to the sun's ultraviolet rays (that's why you see so many RV tires covered). Keep your tires inflated to the indicated maximum pressure on the sidewall and inspect them every trip for signs of wear and damage.

Associated with the tire change modification is the addition of a tire pressure monitoring system (TPMS). This is a standard item on motorhomes and does not apply to truck campers. Some pickup truck manufacturers are including trailer TPMS in their towing packages. Once installed, you can monitor the operator-established pressure and temperature thresholds of your RV's tires. A sudden change in temperature or pressure that exceeds those thresholds will cause an alarm that may give you time to get off the road before the tire blows.

Another popular modification is adding a backup and rear-view monitoring camera. These are standard equipment on motorhomes, and most travel trailers and truck campers are now pre-wired for them (pre-wired means there is a mounting plate, and underneath the mounting plate is a wire connected to the RV's electrical system). In motorhomes, the system is usually hard-wired and in the case of trailers and truck campers, it is a wireless system. The camera mounted on the back of the RV has a built-in transmitter and antenna that transmits the image to a corresponding antenna and monitor to view the image. In some cases, the camera transmits in reverse only while in other cases the camera is on when the vehicle lights are on. Motorhomes can switch between modes, and trailers and truck cameras cannot switch modes unless you install back up lights on the unit and tap into the reverse circuit of the 6-pin or 7-pin connector.

Every RV manufacturer uses the same lock and key combination for its units' outside storage compartments. Every RVer knows this key: CH751. This does not matter to thieves since their preferred method of entry to your outdoor storage compartment is either a crowbar, a prybar, or a large screwdriver. Changing a lock and key is more for peace of mind and convenience than any real measure of increased security. What these locks and keys do is provide enough of a deterrent to keep honest people honest, campground break-ins are exceedingly rare. Your RV is at more risk when you stop at a rest area or big-box store for the night. A common alternative is to install a keyless lock (RVLock for instance) that will set you back around $200.

RVLock also makes keyless locks for your RV's entry door. The upside is you have one less key, and the downside is you may forget the combination! Do not worry, all keyless locks have the option to use a key option as well as a key fob remote.

Interior security is becoming more common among RVers, especially for those who live on the road or have pets. A solution is to install video cameras with the capability of transmitting their views to smart devices. The cameras themselves connect to the RV's Wi-Fi router which in turn relays the video, via the campground's Wi-Fi or an installed cellular device, to your smart device via the internet. Be prepared for high data use if you are not using campground Wi-Fi. Some cameras also have the capability to relay audio from your smart device that allows you to speak to your intruder or pet. An associated modification is a means to monitor internal RV temperature on your smart device through the same connections as the camera. This is extremely helpful when your pet is inside an RV that has lost heating or cooling capability, allowing you time to return to your RV "before it's too late."

Chapter 4: Your Voyage

This chapter focus on various aspects of your voyage such a conducting pre-trip and post-trip inspections, hitching, securing, backing, and using utilities at campgrounds and when boondocking.

Pre-trip and Post-trip inspections

Inspections will save you time, frustration, and money because you will find small problems before they become large problems. What follows is a list of the most crucial items to check. You can find and download exhaustive lists from the internet.

Pre-trip Inspection

- If you are towing a trailer or vehicle, ensure all connections are tight, the safety chains are crossed and connected, the hitch pin is installed and secure, and the 12-volt connector is firmly seated in its socket on the tow vehicle.

- Ensure your truck camper is secure by checking that its tiedowns and shackles are connected and secure. Ensure its 6-pin 12-volt connector is firmly seated in its socket.

- Ensure all lights and signals work (tow vehicle, towed vehicle, and truck camper).

- Check all tires for correct cold pressure and for cracks, bulges, and other damage that could result in a blowout. If you have a TPMS, check pressures with a manual gauge and note differences in those pressures versus sensor pressure. If you have dual rear wheels, ensure the tires are not touching each other.

- Ensure you stowed everything properly.

- Ensure all trailer, truck camper, and towed vehicle windows and doors are closed and locked, and stairs are fully retracted.

- Make sure your slides are retracted fully if you have them (you would be surprised how many people forget this!).

- If you are in doubt on weight, run your setup through a commercial scale to verify your weights.

- Check and top off fluids on the tow vehicle.

- Consult and complete the inspection lists that came with your diesel-pusher or air brake-equipped vehicle.

- If you hook up to a trailer, do a quick tug test, which is attempting to pull away while you are manually applying the trailer's brake (be aware you cannot manually activate a dinghy's brakes). The connections should hold, and the brakes should prevent forward movement.

Post-trip Inspection

The point of a post-trip inspection is to avoid surprises. If you discover something on your post-trip inspection you will have more time to fix it, which will reduce your stress (and most likely everyone else's!). What follows is a list of the most crucial items to check. You can find and download exhaustive lists from the internet.

- Your priority is tire inspection. Ensure your tires have the required pressure, and are without damage such as cracks, tears, and bulges. If you have dual rear wheels, ensure the tires are not touching each other.

- Walk around and check the exterior for damage and missing items. Check underneath for dripping fluids or anything hanging.

- Check your vehicle's fluids because the time to discover it is not right before you leave.

- If you are boondocking and you left with your fresh water tank full, check it because if you leave the overflow valve open, it may siphon itself dry while you are driving.

Towing and Carrying

This section applies to when you are towing a dinghy or travel trailer or carrying a truck camper.

Hitch

Flat-towing is the most common and least expensive method of towing your dinghy. If you are towing your dinghy with a trailer or dolly, then you may need a weight distribution hitch (covered in the next section).

The flat tow hitch connects your motorhome to your dinghy. There are different manufacturers, and they all look and work in the same way. The hitch looks like the letter *A*, where the apex serves as the coupling to the motorhome, and the foot of each leg is attached to points on the towed vehicle's bumper or frame.

You can expect to spend as little as $500 for a HitchMaster to as much as $1,000 for a premium Blue Ox hitch to tow a dinghy safely. There are variations in design so educate yourself on the web and YouTube before you make your decision. Expect to pay another $1,000 for installation which includes the brackets and adapters for the front of your toad, in addition to safety devices and associated electrical wiring. The motorhome brakes must apply the toad brakes, and the motorhome lights and signals must work on the dinghy as well, whether using its factory system or an after-market system.

Using a weight distribution hitch is always a smart idea when towing a trailer, and you *should* use one in the following circumstances:

- The trailer's weight exceeds 50% of the tow vehicle's weight.

- The trailer's tongue weight exceeds the capability of the tow vehicle's receiver.

- Your trailer exceeds the amount prescribed in the tow vehicle's manual.

- When the trailer of the non-weight distributed combination sways.

- When state regulations require it.

There are three types of weight distribution systems: trunnion/round bar, chain, and pivot point projection. The round bar weight distribution hitch is the least expensive, and the pivot point projection weight distribution hitch is the most expensive.

Round bar and trunnion bar weight distribution hitches

Round bar designs like the Husky Centerline, or trunnion bar designs like the Equal-i-zer, work in the same way and vary in price. Round bar designs tend to be less expensive ($300) because they do not usually supply sway control. To control sway, you will need to install devices that minimize sway using friction ($50-$75 each). Trunnion bar designs incorporate anti-sway into the system, so you won't need added devices to gain this functionality. Expect to pay around $600 for a trunnion-bar weight distribution and anti-sway hitch like the Equal-i-zer. While they work exceptionally well to dampen bounce and distribute weight, they are a challenge to adjust, and require time and patience to master. Head over to the world-wide web or YouTube to inform yourself on the process.

Regardless of which design you choose, be prepared for some heavy lifting. The hitch head itself weighs around 70 pounds, and the bars can weigh up to 20 pounds *each*. You must deduct the receiver shank, hitch head, ball, bar, and device weights from m your vehicle's available payload.

Chain weight distribution hitch

Andersen is the only manufacturer of chain-only weight distribution hitches. With this design, the weight distribution function is achieved with chains instead of bars. Increased chain tension yields increased weight distribution. The Andersen hitch has a few benefits. First, the hitch head is aluminum versus iron, so it is much lighter than the round bar and trunnion bar hitch heads (around 30 pounds). Second, round bar and trunnion bars are made from iron and since the Andersen system uses chain, it saves weight here as well (the chains weigh around 1o pounds each). Third, adjusting weight distribution is as easy as tightening or loosening the chain bolts with a socket wrench. Fourth, there isn't any grease to soil your clothes. Lastly, the chains are much easier to stow at your campsite. Expect to pay around $550 for this hitch design.

The Blue Ox Sway Pro weight distribution hitch is a hybrid between the Husky Centerline and Equal-i-zer hitches, and retails for around $700. Flat spring bars handle weight distribution versus round or trunnion bars, and it places tension with a clever fore and aft chain winch system. Friction at the hitch end of the system ensures anti-sway.

Pivot point projection weight distribution hitch

The Hensley Arrow and ProPride weight distribution systems are virtually identical. Jim Hensley, the originator of the pivot point projection concept, sold his design to ProPride and it continues to evolve. Whereas the other weight distribution hitches have the ball as a common pivot point, the pivot point projection hitch shifts that pivot point forward to the rear axle of the tow vehicle. Without getting into a discussion on physics and why this happens, just know that they are extremely effective in *eliminating* sway.

These hitches are very heavy, tipping the scales at about 2oo pounds which counts mostly as payload and a little as tongue weight. The Hensley/ProPride stays attached to the trailer, and the "stinger" (the bar that connects to a receiver in the ProPride) stays attached to the tow vehicle's receiver. The ProPride sells for around $1,700 and the Hensley Arrow sells for around $2,300.

Securing your RV

Chock your wheels when you arrive at your campground to keep fore and aft rocking of your RV to a minimum while also ensuring it is not going to go anywhere. Ensure chocking is the first thing you do when you arrive, and pulling the chocks is the last thing you do when you leave. Use either conventional or X-chocks manufactured by BAL. Use conventional chocks in pairs, one in front and one behind. I recommend the heavy durable rubber chocks over the light plastic ones for durability and security. An alternative to the conventional chock is the X-Chock that fits between the wheels on two-axle units. A ratcheting nut on the unit cranks the legs of the X-Chock out so the feet contact the tires. Once the feet contact the tires make another half revolution to ensure they are tight. You can find conventional rubber chocks for as little as $10, while X-Chocks will set you back about $30 each depending on where you find them.

Backing

One of the most stressful activities of towing is backing. I bring this up in this Voyage section because it is a necessary part of getting from here to there. The most frequent occasion to back up is exiting fuel stations, and in this case, it becomes *the* most stressful part of towing.

If you are towing a vehicle with your RV then it is critically important that you not get yourself into situations where you need to back, because you cannot back up with a dinghy connected. If you find yourself in this position it is not the end of the world; you can disconnect your vehicle, back up, and then reconnect it once you are clear. Your hitch may your ability to backup if you are towing your RV with a vehicle. Hitches that use friction anti-sway devices do not allow backing unless the friction sway control devices are removed, and then you must be very careful to create too much angle between the tow vehicle and RV so you don't bend the friction device.

Backing a trailer is not intuitive. At first, you will tend to turn the wheel in the direction you expect the rear end of the trailer to go when you don't have anything connected. To back a trailer, turn the wheel in the *opposite* direction than you usually turn. When you place your hands at the top of the steering wheel and turn the wheel to the right the trailer goes left, and when you turn the wheel to the left the trailer goes right. That can be very frustrating in the beginning because it takes a lot of mental effort to remember and apply the opposite input rule: *trailer left steer right, trailer right steer left*. The time to learn that mantra is not when you are in a tight spot. Find a parking lot and practice ahead of time.

Tip: Shift your hands to the *bottom* of the wheel when backing. When you move your hands to the right, the trailer, in fact, goes to the right. And when you move your hands left, your trailer moves left. With time and practice, it will become second nature to you and you will be able to move your hands back up to the top of the wheel if you want.

Margin of Safety

You've heard the rule of the two-second interval when following other vehicles. When you drive a motorhome, tow a trailer, or haul a truck camper double that. Your vehicle is going to be slow to respond to inputs such as changing lanes in an emergency or emergency braking. To plan for emergencies, give yourself extra time to react to emergencies. It will be frustrating as cars dart in front of you and take away your safety margin, but ensuring you always keep that margin will help avoid problems by following too closely.

Using Your Utilities

Full Hook-up

A Full hook-up site supplies electricity, water, and sewer. In some parks, you will get CATV as well. Expect to pay a few dollars more for a full hook-up site.

Electricity

On most pedestals, you will find 50 amps, 30 amps, and 20 amps. As discussed earlier, always use a surge suppressor or line conditioner to protect your RV's electrical components.

To connect your rig:

- Before you back into your site, test the outlets to ensure they work. Finding out before you back in is better than afterward, especially if the site was a backing challenge.

- Turn on the breaker for the receptacle capacity you need and use a multimeter, dog bone adapter or surge suppressor with built-in circuit analyzer to ensure it is wired correctly. Turn the power off.

- Back in your rig and ensure your power cable can reach the pedestal. Use your extension if needed.

- Plug your RV's power cable into the surge suppressor or line conditioner (**Note**: The power cable on some RVs disconnect at the pedestal *and* the RV. In this case, plug the cable into your RV after you plug the other end into the surge suppressor or external line conditioner).

- Turn on the breaker at the pedestal, and once the suppressor or line conditioner finishes analyzing the circuit, close the 120-volt service breaker inside the RV. **Note**: While not everyone opens this breaker, it is a good practice when you leave your campsite.

- Throw a bucket over your pedestal or line conditioner if it ends up sitting on the ground to protect it from water intrusion.

<u>Water</u>

As with electricity, check to ensure you have water before you back into your site.

- Sanitize the hose ends, pressure regulator, and campground spigot with a Clorox wipe prior to making any connections.

- Attach the pressure regulator to the spigot, and the hoses to the regulator.

- If you use an inline water filter, connect it between the hose and the regulator because that will remove impurities and tastes from the hose itself.

Tip: Make sure the potable water hose does not run underneath the sewer hose.

Sewer

The biggest payoff for a full-hook-up site comes when it is time to leave. If you have a full hook-up site, you can drain and flush your black water and gray water tanks at your site. If you do not have a full hook-up site, you will need to get in line at the campground dump station to do that chore when you leave. Getting in line is not an ideal solution because very often the line will be long, and tempers can get short (and rain makes them worse!).

Most people are aware of the line and will want to hurry through the job. Hurrying creates stress and makes one prone to mistakes such as remembering to connect the hose to the sewer or the RV *after* you have pulled the dump valve. Also, using a dump station at the end of a weekend typically means that in the interest of being courteous and sensitive to time you neglect to flush your black tank after you have drained it. This practice will lead to odors and solids in your tank. It also can make your tank level sensors inaccurate (no worries, tank sensors are already notoriously inaccurate!).

Some RVers connect their sewer hose when they arrive, and others don't connect it until they are ready to dump. Time and testing will determine which method you prefer. Some campgrounds insist you use sewer hose supports so keep enough on hand to support the hose in its journey from the RV to the sewer drain. A way around this is not to hook up your sewer hose until you are ready to drain your tanks. When the tanks are full, connect the hose then rinse, drain, and remove and stow the hose. Some find this method more convenient because they do not have to carry extra hoses, Y-connectors, or sewer hose supports.

To use your sewer utility:

- Connect the clear elbow to the tank drain, then connect the hose to the elbow. Connect the other end to another elbow and insert this elbow into the sewer drain (**Note**: many campgrounds supply a threaded pipe, so if you have a threaded elbow it can screw on. It is more secure and the best way to connect).

- Do not drain your black tank until it is two-thirds to three-quarters full. The reason is to ensure there is enough material that in turn will supply enough pressure to help the drank drain.

- Drain your gray water tank after you have drained your black water tank. Draining tanks in this order ensures the hose gets a thorough rinse after you have drained the black water tank.

- Do not keep your gray water tank valve open because you need that water to flush the hose.

- Once you have drained the black water tank, flush and drain it a few times until the drainage is clear or close to it.

- More RVs are now coming from the factory with installed internal black water tank flush capability. If you have a black hose connection on the outside of the RV labeled "Black Tank Flush," then you are all set. Connect your black water tank flush hose to the fitting and cycle the water until the drainage is clear.

- If you do not have an installed black water tank flush fitting, then you can use a plastic elbow made for this purpose. The elbow will have a water hose connection with a valve that when open enables the flush. The way it works is it converts incoming water from the pedestal into a high-pressure jet. Once the tank has drained, open the valve and let it spray for a minute, close the valve and let the tank drain, and repeat the process until the drainage is clear.

Dry Camping, Boondocking, and Dispersed Camping

The jury is out on hard definitions for these terms. In general, you are *dry camping* when you are either overnighting somewhere without utilities (e.g., a big box store) or camping without hookups (you can dry camp in a campground with full hook-ups if you choose). Some will tell you that you are *boondocking* when you are dry camping outside of developed campgrounds, (the boondocks) and usually for an extended stay. *Dispersed camping* enters the picture when you are boondocking on federal land. In most cases, dispersed camping does not even look like a campground. When you are dispersed camping you will not find vault toilets, water, a playground, or any other amenity you would associate with a developed campground. In *dispersed camping,* you drive out into the boondocks until you find a nice spot and drop anchor. See chapter 6 on trip planning for more information on this topic. With this type of camping, you are on your own when it comes to water and electricity, and you will need to find a way to deal with your black water and gray water.

For electricity, you will be relying on your 12-volt system unless you have a generator. That means you will not able to use the microwave, television, high dryer, or anything else that uses 110 volts AC. (**Note**: Some RVs come equipped with an inverter that turns 12 volts DC into 110 volts AC. When you use your inverter, it will drain your battery *very* quickly). Solar panels will only recharge your batteries while a generator will recharge your batteries *and* run your 110-volt devices.

Water is going to be a challenge because it is heavy (8.3 pounds per gallon). If you are going out for an extended stay, you will need to ensure that you have enough water and your vehicle(s) are able to carry it. Filling the RV's fresh water tank is often the last thing people think about because their minds tend to be focused on the other items they need to bring such as food, different types of clothing, firewood and gear including ATVs, etc. Fill your fresh water tank(s) first, then weigh your rig so you know who much cargo carrying capacity you have left for all those other things.

Here are some tactics you can employ to stretch your water:

- Take a shower every other day and use disposable wipes on the off days.

- Install a water-saving shower head.

- Use disposable plates and cups that you can burn.

- When you wash dishes use a pot instead of the sink.

- Bring bottled water to drink.

- Bring added water in containers such as hard-sided or expandable potable water totes of assorted sizes.

- Either convert your flush toilet to a composting toilet or bring along a portable flush or composting toilet (each flush of your RV's toilet uses about 2 quarts of water).

- Purchase a portable potable water tank for your pickup truck. To get water from a tote to your RV's freshwater tank use a 12-volt pump or a pump powered by your portable drill (minimal cost and you can find them at Home Depot, Lowe's, Harbor Freight, etc.).

The most challenging issue when camping without utilities is dealing with your black water and gray water. If you are out for just a couple days or you have an RV with large holding tanks (toy haulers specifically) this may not be an issue. For longer stays, you will need to think this through before you get to your location.

Here are some tactics to help extend your stay with regard to human waste. Some RVers who are into boondocking replace their traditional flush-type toilets with composting units. RV composting toilets are expensive; expect to pay upwards of $1,000 for a Nature's Head or Saniflo unit. An alternative composting route is to use a portable composting toilet, and those cost from $20 for a 5-gallon bucket kit up to about $200 for the Thetford 92360 Porta Potti 550E Curve. Non-composting, portable cassette toilets are an alternative; however, they require water in most cases for the flushing system. Another tactic is to boondock in locations where there are vault toilets such as in state and national parks, and state and national forests.

If you are not going to use composting, then you need to consider two things: (1) tank levels, and (2) extending your stay with a portable holding tank.

First, monitor the RV's black water tank level very closely. RV tank sensors are notoriously inaccurate, so if you plan to boondock often upgrade your RV's tank sensors with an upgraded, aftermarket system like those offered by SeeLevel, Level Guard, or Horst (expect to pay around $300).

Second, use a portable holding tank that you can drain at a dump station on the way out or home. Portable holding tanks come in assorted sizes and configurations. Choose one that is most proper given your situation. The thing to keep in mind is that while portable, it will be *heavy*. Tanks range from 10 gallons up to 42 gallons. Using water weight as a base number (8.3 pounds per gallon), the smallest tank will weigh 83 pounds when full, and the largest will tip the scales at 350 pounds. Therefore, the larger tanks come on wheels so they can be towed by a vehicle at extremely low speed to the campground's dump station. Plan appropriately!

Chapter 5: Everyday RV

In this chapter, you will read about what is involved in day-to-day RVing. In the first section, Everyday RV, you will read about RVing with children and pets, how to get a good night's sleep, staying warm and cool, how to pack your clothing, bathing, outdoor activities, buying and storing groceries, cooking inside and outside the RV, the costs of RVing, maintenance and repair, and dealing with breakdowns.

In the second section, Full-Time RVing, you will read about what to consider when you are going to live in an RV, making cash on the road, health care options, Healthcare Options for RVers, how to receive mail and packages while on the road, establishing your domicile, voting, banking, the retirement lifestyle, and preventing loneliness and isolation.

Everyday RV

RVing With Children

The trip itself. A child's body needs a few things: activity, food, and rest, and a schedule. When planning for a trip, make allowances for these, especially activity and schedule. In a motorhome, these are easier because there is room to roam (yes, motorhomes come with seatbelts!). As adults, we can get tunnel vision on our destination at the expense of our children. Children need more frequent stops to work out some of the energy, so do not be stingy with rest stops. Avoid the 'gas, bathroom, food' mantra if you want your children to have an easier time with the trip (which means you will have an easier trip as well!).

Children are active in body and mind. Leverage technology to keep them occupied as you knock down the miles. DVD players, tablets, and smart devices can be your best friend. Ensure you have books, coloring books, and games available for those times when batteries die, or you are out of cell coverage. Let's face it, there is just not a lot of things a person can do when belted into a vehicle at 65 miles per hour.

Plan rest and recreation stops along the way. A tactic on keeping their schedule is to plan for meals around the times you normally eat. You can also capitalize on rest stops and state welcome centers for leg stretching. This will be a challenge for working families on limited schedules but keeping your children on an even keel will make your trip and vacation a lot more enjoyable.

Activities at the location: Plan to do things that will help your children burn off their energy. Shop for campgrounds that have well-outfitted playgrounds and other activities. Bring the bikes, children and bicycles go together. (**Note**: Be safe when you are driving through campgrounds). Today isn't yesteryear. A parent today must be vigilant of the dangers to today's children. Watch your children with either inexpensive campground grade two-way radios, cell phones, or time check-ins. Campgrounds are safe, but you don't want your children on autopilot.

You can overlook health records and immunization records quite easily. Most parents will remember significant illnesses, and thanks to the school system most children will be up-to-date on their immunizations. Health and immunization records become more important the longer your trips become to the point of requiring them when you full time. If your children are taking prescription medication, ensure they have enough on hand for the entire trip including a little more as insurance against delays.

Medical locations: Know the territory you are in, and what medical facilities are available. It does not take more than a couple of minutes to gain situational awareness of medical clinics and pharmacies. If you do that ahead of time, you will be less-stressed (which allows you to think more clearly) when, and if, the time comes to use them.

Health insurance: Shop ahead of time for the clinics that take your type of insurance. This usually isn't an issue with emergent or urgent care, but it is good to know nevertheless, especially considering full-time RVing.

Socialization: This applies more to the extended and full-time RVing community. Full-timing with kids usually happens when they are younger. You do not want your children to grow up isolated, so to build socialization skills stay longer at places when possible (even a few weeks will work wonders). Rallies such as Quartzite are another great means of building socialization skill because they usually last a few weeks and there are a lot of planned and supervised activities for children.

RVing With a Pet

If you have pets, you are probably very attached to them and like to bring them with you on your adventures. What follows are some steps you can take to help you, and them, enjoy the trip.

During your journey, you will need to ensure that you and your pets are safe and comfortable. The key point of safety is ensuring your pets do not interfere with your field of vision and the safe operation of your vehicle. Cats are easy traveling companions simply because of their size. You have noticed them sleeping on the dashboard of the Class A you just passed! That is not a problem when your windshield is six-feet-tall, but when you are in a passenger vehicle with a much shorter windshield (such as Class B, B+, C, and cars and trucks) that cat may prove to be an impediment to your vision. The best way to know is to try it parked in the driveway.

Dogs are a "horse of another color." Dogs tend to be clingy with their owners, more so than cats. Dogs like to be in the middle of the action and close by. That can be dangerous in any traveling situation, whether you are driving an RV or pulling an RV. To keep everyone safe consider a barrier of some sort between you and your fur baby canines, especially if they are larger than the lap dog variety. You can find pet barriers specifically for the type of vehicle you drive when it comes to SUVs and extended cab/crew cab pickup trucks (and many Class B and B+ RVs).

An option is to remove an extra row of seating out of the SUV if the situation permits that will create a living space for your dogs (again, cats are pretty adaptable and are usually free to roam). Newer pickup trucks have foldup rear row seating and folding platforms that create a flat floor in the back row. When you couple that with a mesh barrier you have created a nice traveling arrangement for them. Drop in a couple of doggie beds and they will be quite comfortable, you will be comfortable, and all of you will be safer. **Note**: you can also buy dog harnesses that connect to seat belts. In that case, your fur babies will be occupying a seat versus the floor.

Plan your stops to allow time for your dogs to go to the bathroom and to stretch their legs. They get bored, too, and will need some exercise distraction time. I have never seen a rest stop that did not have an area set aside for animal bathroom breaks. Use them, and please keep your dog on your leash when you do so. Bathroom breaks for your dogs are also good for you because you can use the bathroom and stretch your legs as well. Traveling with these breaks tends to make the trip easier, safer, and not as monotonous.

Be careful about leaving your animals unattended in a parked vehicle. This applies more to hot weather than wintry weather, but the caution stays. If you keep the rule, "when I get out, they get out," you will not run into problems. If that isn't possible, then ensure you leave someone behind to keep the vehicle environment safe and comfortable and switch out with them as needed.

If you plan on overnighting at rest stops then plan for your animals to be a little uptight. There is a lot of action in rest stops due to vehicles coming and going all night long. Your pets will be vigilant, and in the case of dogs, will alert you to every one of those events. If you plan to stop at a big-box store for the night, ensure you pick up your pet and do not stake them out. While these stores and restaurants are generous in allowing overnighting, you do not want the appearance that you are setting up camp. Also, ensure you check your campgrounds to ensure they allow pets, and further, they allow your breed of pet. Some campgrounds do not allow larger dogs with bad reputations such as Rottweilers, Pit Bulls, Dobermans, etc.

Ensure you are up to date on your animal's health, they are tagged properly, and their immunization records are readily available. If you are boondocking out on dispersed land, ensure you have proper flea and tick prevention. Keep paper copies where you can get to them easily if asked for by law enforcement. You can also store them as PDFs so you can print as needed (some folks travel with small portable printers).

When you finally get to your site, the biggest thing you can do to be a good neighbor is to be respectful of others, more in the case of dogs than cats.

If you are going to keep dogs outside with you,

• keep them on a leash or tethered to an immovable object,

• ensure their lead is not long enough to get into the street or to other campsites,

• ensure they have water and shade, and

- ensure you stay with them (campgrounds, as a rule, do not allow unattended pets, so you cannot stake out your dog and go to the waterpark).

Now a note about barking. Some breeds are hypervigilant. You have heard them barking at every pine cone and leaf rustled by the wind. Incessant barking is annoying when people look for quiet and solitude. You can train dogs not to bark, and you can also use anti-bark collars that deliver a sound, vibration, or small shock when the collar's unit detects a bark (or soon-coming bark). Campgrounds will expel campers who have dogs that won't stop barking.

While traveling with pets can be quite enjoyable, there are downsides, especially in the case of dogs. Separation anxiety can lead to destruction of property as they either try to claw their way through the door, or chew on everything in the RV because they miss you, and they are in an unfamiliar environment. Chewing is their way to displace their anxiety. There a few ways to help your pet cope with uncertainty and anxiety while traveling. One way is veterinarian-prescribed medications to help take the edge off when you leave them unattended in the RV. Another way is to gradually desensitize them to your absence, especially while traveling. Try leaving them inside for progressively longer periods while you are outside. Then graduate to leaving them inside while you take progressively longer walks. Always return after each test to look for evidence of damage before moving on to a longer test. Leave a variety of chew toys behind for them to cope with their anxiety and to focus their energy when they get bored.

Some RVers install video cameras so they can monitor their pets via smartphone apps. Some of these allow audio so you can see and hear what they are up to. In some cases, you can even speak back to them which gives you the opportunity for supplying correction, reassurance, or praise. To capitalize on these cameras, you will need to have reliable Wi-Fi. Do not forget another device and app to monitor the temperature.

Bring your pet's normal food and pack enough for the duration of the trip plus a couple of extra servings. If you full-time, choose a brand with national distribution. Scan your destination ahead of time for recommended veterinarians and pet boarding. This can pay big dividends if your pet becomes ill or if you need to leave them for boarding for some reason (such as day trips where pets are not welcome).

Lastly, plan dog-friendly activities such as walks and hikes. It is a great exercise for them, reduces their boredom, and helps them to be more relaxed around the campsite.

Getting a Good Night's Sleep

Getting a good night's sleep can be a challenge on the road if you are a light sleeper. Noise and light are the two culprits that will keep you awake. RVs are not known for their sound-insulating qualities, and campgrounds are not the quietest places until quiet hours begin (usually around 10 pm). If you like to get to bed earlier than quiet hours, I suggest a few things. First, book a spot away from playgrounds. Many RV spots are also along major thoroughfares, so finding a spot at the farthest point away from them will help attenuate the sound more.

Another thing you can do is find a spot that allows the bedroom of the unit to be on the opposite side of the unit from where the noise source is. For instance, if the bedroom is in the back as in motorhomes, try to park with the front of the coach pointing towards the noise source to put a little extra distance between you and the source. Many RVs use bedroom doors that can help block the noise, so capitalize on this if you can. Also, windshields are made from tempered glass (two layers with a plastic sheet in between), and that makes them surprisingly good sound deadeners. You can also buy an ambient sound (white noise) generator and run it by your bed, or even a white noise app and run it through the RVs entertainment system.

Get used to large diesel engines, the sound of airbrakes being set and released, and the inevitable truck traffic that goes with it If you stop at a rest stop or truck stop for the night. Some folks find that the idling diesels create a relaxing white noise of their own and enjoy it. Reefer trailers add to that because they have their own diesel engines that run the freezer units. Remember that if you are stopping in this circumstance your fur babies (and you) will be hypervigilant, which means sleep will be fleeting for all of you. As a last resort try ear plugs.

Light is also a challenge if you like to nap in the daytime or go to bed before the sun sets (a frequent occurrence in northern latitudes). Some RVs come from the factory with day/night shades that tend to create a darker internal environment than your typical mini-blind. Even with those pulled, it will not be dark. If you need darkness, then swap out your mini-blinds or day/night shades with room darkening shades. If you have a crank-open fan where you sleep, you may need to buy a baffle for it. RV doors are short to allow for circulation because there are no return vents in an RV. If you close your doors off, then your heat and air conditioning will not work efficiently which means a cold sleeping area when it is cold outside, and a warm sleeping area when it is warm outside.

Staying Warm and Cool

The primary means of staying warm in your RV is by running its heat. All RVs use propane for heat, and some have added "fireplaces" that are 110-volt AC electric heaters. The byproducts of propane heat are carbon monoxide and moisture. The best way to cut carbon monoxide and reduce moisture (and thereby condensation on the interior surfaces) is to crack a window or vent.

Note: Replace carbon monoxide detectors and smoke alarms every five years.

If you are at a full hookup site and your RV has electric heat, run that to reduce propane cost. If you are boondocking, be aware that your heating system uses 12-volts DC to run the furnace blower. A chilly night can suck your battery dry, so consider alternatives to your onboard heat system such as flannel pajamas, bed sheets, added blankets, and vent insulators (foam inserts for your vents). Some RVers will also use propane space heaters like a Mr. Buddy or Little Buddy that use less propane and do not affect the house battery. Ensure you turn these off before going to sleep.

There are measures you can take to increase the efficiency of your RV's cooling system. First, inspect your system to see if it uses ducting, and if it does, tape all the joints with HVAC tape (not duct tape). Second, make panels to mount on the inside of our windows to keep the sun out or to reflect its rays (Reflectix is a top choice among RVers). Third, park the refrigerator side of the RV away from the sun (it helps the refrigerator run cooler). Fourth, consider a screen attachment for the awning to keep afternoon sun at bay (they cost as little as $50). Fifth, tolerate a little warmer RV. Sixth, replace the analog on/off thermostat with a digital thermostat (around $50 from most big-box stores). The digital thermostat typically helps your HVAC system run more efficiently because it maintains a more stable temperature. Seventh, bring a fan to circulate air inside the RV. Eighth, consider replacing the OEM vent fans with high capacity, reversible vent fans (expect to pay $50 for a conventional on/off unit, and up to $200 for a thermostatically-controlled, reversible, remotely controlled fan).

Note: Do not rapidly cycle your air conditioning unit thinking it will cool more efficiently. Wait at least two minutes before starts because you burn out the compressor. Short-cycling the unit will also lead to ice build on the evaporator coils which will in turn reduce its ability to cool.

Clothing

Here is where you can make life easier. Keep a set of clothing in the RV so you are not hauling clothing back and forth. The key items are outdoor wear such as jackets, coats, raincoats, camping shoes and hiking boots. Space can be a premium, so the amount of clothing you leave in your RV will vary depending upon your type of RV.

Bathing

Get Used to Navy Showers! Say goodbye to long showers in an un-modified RV. Even if you hook up to campground sewer, you still must contend with the ability of your water heater to supply enough hot water for a longer shower. The most common water heater is a 6-gallon, propane-fired unit. Le to enjoy a continuous hot shower for about 2 minutes. The challenge is ensuring you have enough hot water for a *complete* shower. If you take your shower this way you will not run out of hot water.

Here is how to take a Navy shower:

- You should be standing there in your birthday suit ready to go. You do not want to take time and waste precious hot water while you disrobe.

- If you are hooked up to fresh water in the campground, start by turning on the cold water and gradually add hot water till it feels good to you.

- As soon as the temperature is good, get in and rinse yourself head to toe, and then shut the water off on the shower head (all RVs come equipped this way).

- Wash your hair and body all in one shot, then rinse.

Note: It can take a long time to get shampoo out of long hair, longer than the hot water you will have available to you. You may want to wash your hair on alternate days or alternate times to ensure you have enough hot water.

To move beyond navy showers, manufacturers are installing ten-gallon tanks, and augmenting gas with electricity. A combination gas-electric, ten-gallon water heater will yield a longer hot shower because the gas and electricity work together to keep the temperature higher longer. The electric side of the water heater only runs on shore power.

Outdoor Activities

What does one do when parked? This can be quite disorienting for full-timers who have worked their entire lives. The question seeks to find activities one can pursue. There are as many ways to occupy your time with an RV as in your home, with the exception perhaps of yard work! Hike, ride bicycles, sight-see and go to shows, etc. Do not forget the time-honored American campground evening tradition: a nice, toasty fire to sit around while you enjoy the beverage of your choice.

RV Cooking

There are minor differences between cooking in an RV and cooking in your home. What makes it different is space to prepare, serving it, and storing of left-overs. At one end of the spectrum is the Class A motorhome. In many cases, these kitchens rival the kitchens in your home. They have fully-outfitted residential appliances and storage capacity, and plenty of room to prepare, serve, and store meals. On the other side of the spectrum are Class B/B+ and Truck Camper kitchens that consist of a one- or -two burner propane cooktop, little space, and tiny refrigerators. In larger units with larger refrigerators, you will be able to keep enough food on hand to serve many meals, while in the smallest units you will only be able to store enough food for as few as one or two meals. Some RVs have outside kitchens with mini-refrigerators that allow you to expand your storage and cooking space there (**Note**: mini-refrigerators are 110-

volts AC only, so you won't be able to run them unless you are in a motorhome).

Cooking inside. Whether you cook inside or not depends on the time of year, the size of our family, and what meals you plan. When people get away for the weekend in their RVs, they usually do not plan elaborate meals. That is even more so when planning meals in smaller RVs with limited storage and preparation space.

Kitchen space is a premium, so multitask your cookware. You can use cast iron skillets on the stove top, in an oven, or outside on a grill or grill oven. Instapots can slow cook, or serve as a rice cooker, egg cooker or pressure cooker. You can sauté and brown, bake a cake, steam veggies, warm items up, or even sterilize.

Tip: Run your vent fan while you cook. It is a guarantee you will set off the smoke alarm because of the heat that comes from cooking in a small space like an RV. The smaller the RV, the greater the tendency for this to happen.

Cooking outside. Some folks use the grates that come on campground fire pits. If that is your case, clean the grill and use aluminum foil. Some RVers also use outside cooking appliances. Some RVs come with external propane connections and grill mounts for included propane grills. Others have outside kitchens that expand your cooking ability and include amenities such as induction cook tops. In many cases, these outside appliances are usually low-powered, but enough for a couple. When cooking for more people, you will need to start thinking along the Camp Chef line of outdoor grills and appliances.

RV Costs

RVing can be inexpensive, or it can be expensive depending on your planning and tastes.

The cost of RV ownership serves as the first "layer" of cost. You must consider insurance, maintenance and repair, and breakdowns into the cost of the RV lifestyle. Obtaining insurance for a travel trailer or truck camper is at the lowest end of the cost spectrum, and the particular cost and size of your RV will cause those rates to fluctuate: higher cost units will occupy the more expensive end of the spectrum, lower cost units on the less expensive end of the insurance cost spectrum. As an example, an Airstream trailer will be cost far more to insure than a Surveyor trailer of the same length. Class B and B+ motorhomes will be less expensive to insure because their cost and risk level is much lower than larger motorhomes. When you move up to a C, Super C, or Class A motorhome, insurance rates get extremely high because they cost more to buy, and they are larger, heavier, and require higher skill sets to drive. All these elements combine to create more risk for the insurance company (like you hitting lower things like bridges, windstorms tipping your RV over, etc.).

The next layer of cost consists of modifications and accessories. If you are buying a smaller motorhome like a B or B+, you will not have too many modifications on your list. If you are buying a C, Super C, or Class A and intend to be mobile at your campsite (and your RV is large enough), you may intend to haul another vehicle. You will then think through the cost of towing/trailering a dinghy.

Towing an RV also includes cost. The larger the RV, the more preparation and modification the vehicle needs. The smallest RVs will not need any tow vehicle modifications at all, but as they get larger, they will require towing mirror add-ons if not equipped, brake controllers, weight distribution hitches and anti-sway devices, vehicle leveling modifications, trailer TPMS, observation cameras, etc. In some cases, you will need a bigger vehicle so that is a big cost by itself.

Truck campers require truck preparation as well. You cannot simply drop a camper in the bed.

Installation of straps and turnbuckles are required to carry the camper safely. The truck may also require suspension and tire modifications.

The third layer focuses on the cost of traveling, such as where you stay along the road, eating, fuel costs, tolls, etc. If you are on a multi-day journey going to or coming from the campground, you can overnight at hotels, campgrounds, or free places like rest stops or truck stops to save cash. You can factor eating along the way as a trip expense or consider it an extra expense. You can hold down cost by ensuring you have enough groceries to make your own meals and couple them with rest breaks.

If you are buying a motorhome that will be a sobering experience to fuel up, especially in the diesel-powered Class A and Super C motorhomes. Class B/B+ and C motorhomes will be a little more friendly because they are gasoline-powered, and gasoline is typically less expensive than diesel fuel. If you plan to tow anything, whether it is an RV or a dinghy, your fuel costs will increase because your fuel mileage will drop. If you are in a part of the country with tolls, and depending on your type of RV, you may see higher travel costs from tolls. Tolls are usually indexed to the number of axles and class of vehicle, so you will not pay anything more while carrying a truck camper than when you are traveling without it, or when traveling in a Class B/B+ motorhome. In all other cases, you will pay more tolls.

The fourth layer consists of all the costs related to staying at your destination. Where you stay will have a dramatic effect on destinations cost. You can choose to stay at an amenity-packed RV resort that satisfies the tastes and styles of high-end class A RV drivers, or you can choose to stay for free on public land such as Bureau of Land Management reserves. Private campgrounds will be more expensive and offer more amenities such as full hook-ups and playgrounds than less expensive state parks that offer few amenities (vault toilets and shower houses). Public land offers no amenities except for fresh air, no noise, beautiful views, and proximity to nature. Note that the further you move off-grid, the cheaper it becomes to stay and the more expensive it becomes to equip your RV to do so. Sometimes you can get a discount on longer stays, and the time of year impacts cost (a week at Disney Fort Wilderness in January will cost $500, and a week in May could run as much as $1000).

A way to reduce cost is by working if your situation in life allows it. Working from your RV in the knowledge sector is a wonderful way to cut destination, but it carries its own costs such as reliable computing and communication. As outlined previously, communication and data are the expensive parts of the equation. If you are going to work in this sector, then plan on spending extra cash to ensure you can communicate when needed and with enough bandwidth.

Many who do work on the road own hotspots from different carriers depending on the part of the country in which they are staying. Do not forget the cost of preparing workspace in your RV. You'll need a flat space with enough room to sprawl a little bit, a reliable power supply (think UPS here), a line conditioner, and a means to store it all while traveling. The cost incurred depends on how elaborate you wish to be, and your work style. Compare the *Traveling Robert* and *I Love RV Life* YouTube channels to see how great the variation can be while still carrying out the same ends.

Maintenance and Repair

Maintenance: Owning an RV and extending its life and serviceability is not any different than doing the same thing with a lawn mower or car. Its life and reliability come down to how well you take care of it. Start with routine inspection and make a list. Check every system periodically. The point is to spot small problems before they become big problems. Of all that can go wrong, water intrusion is the worst, so take your time looking for its evidence. Next, set up a maintenance schedule of what tasks you should do, and when you need to do them. A fitting example is annual brake and axle bearing inspections for travel trailers. Make sure you have all the materials on hand for periodic maintenance on rubber seals, roofs, air conditioning units, bearings, etc. When the size goes up, maintenance gets more complicated. Most of us do not have the ability or space to do the more meticulous maintenance required for a Class A diesel pusher, so ensure you have enough money in the budget to have these things done.

Repair: Repairs are unplanned or planned. Planned repair is always less expensive than unplanned repair, especially when you are in a remote location. Some RVers are not handy, and that is you then try to be a little handier. RVs are boxes screwed together and attached to frames that go down the highway at 65+ miles per hour. The whole thing is going to flex, and something is going to break at some point regardless of how much money you spend on the unit in the beginning. That is the nature of RVing.

You can lower repair cost by taking on some repairs yourself. Ensure you have a basic toolkit and inform yourself. There plenty of books, websites, and YouTube videos to coach you through many situations you will meet. Accept that there are some things that you cannot handle with a basic toolkit and will require help, for instance some engine repair especially on the newer motorhome engines. Be aware of where you try repairs. You can get away with minor repair in a campground, but the more involved it becomes the less of a chance you will be able to carry it out it in a campground during a short stay. You will need to communicate with the office to be sure. Also, if you are making repairs, you will need to make sure you have the time to do it before the campground staff ask you to make room for another RVer.

Breakdowns

The best thing you can do about breakdowns is to plan for and expect them to happen. Having a good response plan means reducing your stress, increasing your ability to keep a cool head, and thinking more clearly.

First, ensure you have an adequate roadside assistance plan. Most new RVs are delivered with one year of roadside assistance by Coach-Net. Before it expires, investigate other plans offered by Good Sam, Family Motor Coach Association, AAA, and others such as your current insurance provider. These plans will include services for lockouts, fuel and fluids delivery, tire changing and replacement, towing, food, lodging, gap replacement, etc. (Note: plans vary in services, so do your homework and choose the one that gives you the most bang for our buck given your tolerance level).

Second, ensure you have a fire extinguisher and breakdown kit that is readily available. As a minimum, the breakdown kit should have reflective, high-visibility triangles or cones, a high-visibility vest, and some means to jack up the RV should you need to change a tire. Some people also carry a readily-available tool kit to handle repairs quickly (do not forget your duct tape!)

Third, move your rig as far off the traveled road as you can and into a safe place, and get out of the vehicle while you are waiting for help. There is no guarantee that a passing vehicle will not strike your rig because it is parked in the breakdown lane.

Fourth, expect to wait at least an hour for assistance. Yours is not the only case your roadside assistance provider is working on. It is also quite likely that whoever receives the call will need to gather the proper supplies. The last delay is travel time. It may take a while to get to you if you are in a remote location.

Note: You may not have cellular service, especially if you are in a remote location. Consider a satellite-based option that allows emergency contact from brands such as Garmin, Spot, ACR, DeLorme, or RescueMe. The Garmin and Spot units will cost from $150 for the Spot Messenger up to around $400 for the Garmin InReach. The other units are emergency locator beacons that do not provide voice or text capability, so they are not as versatile.

Fifth, be wary of aid given by other motorists. Some will be honest and have the skills you need to get you back on the road. Then there are honest and helpful people with no skills that can at least get help if you are not able to get help on your own (out of cellular service area). Watch out for those who have ill-intention in mind. Unfortunately, that is our default assessment today, so we need to be careful. Pay attention to your intuition and do not be afraid to refuse help.

Sixth, consider your options. If you are in a motorhome and you are not towing a vehicle, your options are limited. If it breaks down you are stuck, even if you are towed to a metropolitan area. You will need to rent a vehicle in addition to finding a hotel until your RV is fixed. If you are towing a dinghy with your RV at least you have mobility. If you are towing a travel trailer or carrying a camper and your tow vehicle breaks down, at least you have a place to stay and can make meals while you work out the mobility challenge. If your travel trailer or truck has an issue that requires repair you still have your tow vehicle, so you only need to find lodging and take care of meals.

Tip: Keep your campground phone numbers handy so you can let them know about a delay and share your location on your devices so family and friends can follow your journey. They can spot if you stop at an unplanned place for an extended length of time.

Seventh, keep emergency food and water readily available. If you are stranded, keeping warm and cool is especially important, especially if you have children or pets. If you have another vehicle in the combination, you can use it as a lifeboat (just ensure you are safe when you do it!).

Full-Timing

What to Consider When You're Going to Live in an RV

Planning. Successful full-timing depends on a plan. Ensure you follow the guidelines below for a smooth transition. The biggest consideration is what to do with your sticks-and-bricks house. Some RVers keep it and either pay for someone to maintain it or rent it out to others who will take care of it in their absence. The advantage is a home base and an appreciating asset if needed. Other RVers sell it to finance their RV and their upcoming lifestyle. (**Note**: If you sell, ensure you safeguard the proceeds to buy another residence when you need to come off the road).

The other major consideration is deciding what to do with your belongings. Keeping important mementos aside, some RVers sell or give way everything they have, and others keep some back in storage for when and if they come off the road. Only you can decide the path you will take. The key to avoiding a costly mistake is by taking your time with the process.

Making Cash on the Road

If you plan to make cash on the road with a business or by taking part in the gig economy, then prove that you can make money that way before you leave. Consider writing, photography, or other ways to generate income that does not require "going into the office." Many full-timers take part in work camping, which means exchanging work for a place to park the RV and utilities. This is quite common, especially among retirees. Consult agencies such as the National Park Service and U.S. Army Corps of Engineers for opportunities. A web search will also turn up many options.

Healthcare Options

I spoke about this with children, so I will be brief here. Most people who retire and hit the road do it while they are still healthy. You will find most of full-timers are Baby boomer and Gen X'ers in their 50s to 70s, although many millennials are now hitting the road with their young families. Some are healthy enough in their 80s.

Full-timers set up a domicile to where they return periodically. Those domiciles are where they get their routine medical and dental care. From there they will get their "clean bill of health" and what they need to head back out. For events that pop up along the way, urgent care and emergency care will be the choice. The challenge can be prescription meds while you are underway, so choosing to have medications refilled at national chains are a choice so they are always available (Target, Wal-Mart, Walgreens as an example). You can also use mail-order pharmacies when you know where you will be and when you will be there. Research your destination ahead of time and know what is available for routine, urgent, and emergency medical, dental, and pharmacy support. Call to verify insurance coverages, and ensure you have enough cash on hand (or room on our credit cards) for deductibles. If you really like your doctors, ask them if they have a referral for the area to which you are traveling.

Establishing Domicile

You can use the address of family for friends, or you can choose a state that allows RVers to domicile. All you need is a street address, so a post office box is not a legitimate legal residence. Choosing a state can be huge due to the impact on income taxes, insurance, vehicle taxes, sales taxes, etc. All the items that line up with state residency are driver's license, vehicle registration and insurance, voting, and health insurance. The states more chosen are those that do not have income tax (e.g., Alaska, Florida, Nevada, South

Dakota, Texas, Wyoming, and Washington). Florida, Texas, and South Dakota are the most popular because they don't have income tax and they are flexible on residency requirements. It bears repeating that for whatever state you choose as a domicile, all the other critical elements spoken of to this point will need to line up under it.

Mail

Knowing where you are going to be and when you will be there is critical if you expect to receive prompt written correspondence. Post office boxes are an excellent choice if you return with predictability (USPS and UPS especially). You can use mail forwarding, but that can be tedious and unreliable, especially when you are changing locations often. A popular choice is using a family address and they can then send mail to you in batches at the campground you are at or to the post office box you are using. A way for shorter trips is to simply hold your mail. There are also companies such as Traveling Mailbox that specialize in mail and package forwarding. You can expect to pay $15 to $60 per month for this service.

Voting

Registering for voting is one of the greatest reasons to establish a domicile. Once you have established it, you can then vote absentee.

Banking

Establishing bank accounts and credit cards requires a home address (Patriot Act). Choose a bank with national bricks-and-mortar locations in case you need to go in or use an ATM to receive or deposit cash (e.g., Bank of America or Wells Fargo). You can also use online banks that tend to be less expensive (e.g., Ally Bank, Capital One, etc.), cash, or refillable credit cards. Your preferred method of banking determines how money goes in and how it goes out.

Paying bills online and online check deposit through the bank's app are convenient ways to move money into and out of your bank account. Credit cards can be handy but watch how you use them, so you do not overspend. Full-timing requires meticulous financial care. If you are going to use credit cards routinely, take care to notify that company of changes in routine.

Tip: Split up your money into different banks. It can be cumbersome but remember you will be capitalizing on an online environment that can be fickle. Having more than one bank gives you redundancy, especially when you really need cash.

RV Lifestyle in Retirement

Be careful with your standard of living because you may be living on a fixed income. Make some cash in the gig economy if needed, so don't burn bridges if you work in that sector. A key strategy is to be content with less (you are already there if you have sold your house and all your belongings). Instead of dinner and show, consider lower-cost options such as community classes or outdoor activities and hobbies. Be ready for a lot of free time, so keeping routines and establishing new ones before you hit the road will ensure you stay active.

Prevent Loneliness and Isolation

This is not an issue if you currently are a hermit! If you aren't then you will need to find a way to make connections. Socialization is just as important as it is for children. Participate in RV-focused rallies (e.g., Quartzite, Forest River Owners Group, etc.) or groups and rallies you support in current hobbies and interests (e.g., Honda Owners Group, Harley Owners Group, astronomy, geology, birding, etc.). The bottom line is to continue seeking out ways to connect with others.

Chapter 6: What to Know, and Where to Go

In this brief chapter, you will learn about Choosing a Destination and How to Get There.

Choosing a Destination

RVParky: This app is an RV park directory written by an RVer with user-generated reviews, images, and information. It works with GPS and displays RV parks, campgrounds, and RV-friendly stores on a clickable map, and it works equally well on mobile devices or computers.

Free Camping: This is an RV community-driven app and website that helps you find user-reviewed free camping sites of all types on a clickable map, then uses its built-in trip planner to map your trip. You can also filter results by amenities desired. Free Camping is free; however, you will need to create an account to get the most benefit from it.

Reserve America: Reserve America is a free membership-based app and website. It is unique in that you can search for, find, and *reserve* a spot within the app including hiking trips, day-use facilities, lodging, and other outdoor activities like fishing trips. It is one-stop shopping.

RVLife: A subscription mobile device app that helps you find a campground, fine-tune it with multiple levels of clickable amenities, read the reviews, and map the trip from within the app. A unique attribute of this app is the downloadable map for when you are out of the range of cell towers.

Recreation.gov: Federal facility directory website and app that draws from 12 federal agencies such as the National Forest Service, National Park Service and Bureau of Land Management. This resource also has a trip builder that helps you to search for a site across 3,500 federal facilities.

How to Get There

RV Trip Wizard: Find campgrounds, points of interest, determine cost and set driving times and distances with this web-based application. This application is different in several ways from other trip planers. First, Whereas RV trip planners tend to show only the campgrounds affiliated with their respective publishers, RVTW shows all campgrounds. Second, it uses a map interface to set driving time and distance via concentric user-determined circles. You determine how large the circles are based upon your endurance. Third, it has cost monitoring features built in that allow you to factor tolls, fuel, campgrounds, food and other costs to watch the overall trip cost.

Copilot: This is a highly-recommended, version-specific navigation and traffic app for either cars, trucks or RVs that requires an annual $29.95 membership. The app looks like a conventional GPS unit, and allows for out-of-cell tower use via downloadable offline maps that work with the GPS chip in your device.

While you are traveling

GPS units: Many RVers prefer to use a separate GPS device for their travels. There are many from which to use, and RVers tend to choose the RV-specific units that provide live-traffic capability. The benefit of using stand-alone GPS units is they usually have much larger screens that are not obscured by sunlight, they do not tie up your smart device, nor are they dependent upon either cell tower service or downloadable maps that can clog up your device. Expect to pay upwards of $300 for premium units such as the Garmin RV 770 LMT-S or the Rand McNally RVND 7730 LM.

Map: The *Rand McNally Motor Carrier's Atlas* is the RVers best off-line friend. It is the same atlas commercial trucker drivers use, and it is extremely helpful in showing roads with weight, height, axle, and length limitations. Expect to pay around $20 for this atlas in softcover format, or around $75 for laminated, spiral-bound versions. The benefit of using this is to "sanity-check" your GPS, to see the entire route at once, to enable less-stressful on-the-fly travel planning.

iExit: This is a free, web-based and mobile device application that watches your location on the highway and displays upcoming gas, food, shelter and rest stops by highway exit number. When you click on an exit, the app lists its services including the price of fuel. It connects to other apps such as Yelp and Google Maps, so you can click to review or click to get directions. You can either discover and map the stops ahead of time or find yourself on the map via your mobile device's location services. If you are going to keep an app going while on the road, this is the one.

Rest Stops: This app enables you to find a rest stop by drilling down by state, highway, and direction of travel. Once found, you can get directions with Waze, Google Maps, or Apple Maps from within the app. The app also shows RV dump stations.

Sidebar: Temporary/Overnight Stops

Big Box Overnighting: Call ahead, introduce yourself to the manager if you can, buy something while you are there, do not run your generator or kick out your slides, pick up after yourself, and park out of the way. The most common stops are Wal-Mart, CostCo, Sam's, Cabela's, Camping World, Cracker Barrel, and truck stops.

Conclusion

Thank you for making it through to the end of *The RV Experience*. Let's hope it was informative and it provided you with all of the tools you need to achieve your goals in pursuing the RV lifestyle.

Choosing an RV is your biggest decision, and everything that follows is guided by it. You will not find the perfect RV. What you *will* find is an RV that satisfies the most items on your list for the money you want to spend. From there you will supply it, outfit it, and modify it to get it as close as you can to the perfect RV as you imagined. Let safety and light weight be your guide.

Your RV is the key that opens the door to adventure. Your adventure may be in top-tier RV resorts, amenity-packed family campgrounds, state and national parks, or out in the boondocks. Finding these locations, planning the journey, and staying on track is now easier than ever when you use web-based and smart device technology.

It is not enough to simply read the book; it is now time to use it as a guide in your journey. Print the chapters and mark on them, number them, and convert them to checklists you can follow along the way. Enjoy your journey as you build memories for a lifetime.

If you found this book useful in any way, a review is always appreciated!

Made in United States
North Haven, CT
23 March 2022